Know Your Chakras

An Introduction to Energy Medicine

How chakras affect your physical, emotional and spiritual health

Helen Chin Lui
Certified Energy Medicine Practitioner,
Certified Reflexologist &
Usui Reiki Master/Teacher

Helen Chin Lui
All rights reserved.
ISBN-10: 1981267956
ISBN-13: 978-1981267958

Dedication

To everyone who wants to reclaim their powerful energy!

Acknowledgements

Thank you to each person who believed in me, supported my vision, and encouraged me every step of my journey. Without a team, there wouldn't be the Healing Place LLC and Healing Place Energy School LLC. Every person's role is significant. Many have contributed countless hours to grow the Healing Place from a hands-on healing business to a global resource of online classes. I believe this is only the beginning of what is to come.

Let me take a curtsy and acknowledge in *print and out loud*:

My husband, Richard Lui, the love of my life, who has unrelentingly supported me on my journey since 1971. Richard encouraged me to do this healing work even when I wanted to quit. He recognized my life's purpose better than I did and wouldn't let me give up, even when I cried hours of tears while complaining that the work was so hard and no one understood what I did. Thank you.

My sons, Jeffrey and Brian Lui, for being two great guys who taught me never to give up; both sons have contributed tremendously to my growth and my knowledge; from how to deal with health issues that had no answers to continually being a source of courage and inspiration. We learned we don't have to be at the mercy of conventional methods of healing. We HAVE choices! They were always there with kind words, and they cooked for me when I was too tired. Thank you, my boys.

My puppies, Kirby, Milo, and Tito, who make me smile. They tell me when to take breaks by asking me to walk them and afterwards, I can come back to the computer refreshed. I'll give you a cookie later. Thank you, puppies.

My sisters, Polly Chin-Ahern and Betty Chin, who have been my life-long cheerleaders. Thank you.

My brothers, Jan Chin who passed in 2011 from lung cancer at the age of 54 and my brother Kenny, who is still with us. Thank you.

My mother, Fay Kam Chin, who forced me to learn patience and compassion; I wouldn't be who I am if it weren't for you. Thank you.

My Dad, Thomas Shee Fun Chin, who passed away too soon. Thank you for having the courage to leave China and making a life in USA.

My assistant, Amanda Lohnes, whom I have known since 2003. I hired her as my intern at the last job I had before I began the Healing Place, and she is now the Healing Place's proofreader, content designer, and editor. I love that when I write something and Amanda doesn't comment (which is extremely rare, I know I did a good job. Thank you.

My marketing consultant, Lavinia Jones, for taking my business to the next level and being a voice of reason when I get into a tizzy. Thank you for being patient with me. Thank you for your wisdom. Thank you for answering my emails at 2AM GMT time. Thank you.

My webmaster, Jonathan Shubow, for designing my websites. I have known Jon since we were in seventh grade. Thank you for yelling at me when I didn't understand what SEO was.

I thank the thousands of clients who have honored the Healing Place by trusting us to help them find relief from their chronic digestive problems, chronic pain from autoimmune diseases, and hormone imbalances. I want to give a big thanks to Stanley Elkerton, my first client. As an engineer, I had to educate Stan how Reflexology would benefit and help him. He was always catching colds. We were able to knock down the number of colds he caught from four to maybe one a year. Thank you for believing and trusting me.

I thank my tens of thousands of readers on social media (Twitter, Facebook, YouTube, LinkedIn, and Instagram who follow, share, and like the Healing Place. Thank you for your support.

Most importantly, I thank God for giving me the guidance and the courage to established a business in 2006 when no one knew what Reflexology and energy healing were. Thank you God.

The Healing Place wouldn't be the Healing Place without your support. Thank you all for being a part of my life and being a blessing to me.

Preface

My journey of healing started when my son was young and became chronically ill. A variety of health complications plagued him for more than fifteen years.

He became sick in the early 90's and, his doctors either didn't know or didn't understand the complexities of his illnesses. The only option at the time was a list of medications that no 14-year-old child should have to take just to get temporary relief.

In 1995, I made it my life's mission to help him to break his pain cycle with natural remedies, including the alternative healing of Reiki. We changed his diet, eliminating all gluten and processed foods, and increased his fruit and vegetable intake. We added supplements like omega oils and Vitamin B complex for digestive health. To help relieve his stress and anger, we enrolled him into a variety of school sports, and we did a lot of talk therapy.

As of today, my son has broken his chronic pain cycle and is in a better place. His life is not always perfect; he still has days when he is not feeling well, but he is no longer tormented daily with unrelenting chronic pain.

Why have I chosen to write this book? Energy healing has made such a dramatic and positive difference in the lives of my loved ones and in my own life, and I sincerely want to help others to break their pain cycle and stop their suffering, too. When my young son suffered from years of unrelenting physical and emotional pain and our only solution at the time was medication. My husband and I watched helplessly, praying that the doctors were choosing the right medical regimen for him. Many times, it was a guessing game and very frustrating trying to hit upon just the right combination of therapies and medications that would help him to heal. With traditional medicine, we saw our son improve, but not enough for him to live a life full of joy and good health; and the underlying causes of his problems went unaddressed. There were too many questions that went unanswered. Many of the procedures and medications were done on a trial-and-error basis--some helped, and some caused more harm.

Instead of waiting for doctors' resolutions that never came, I decided to take the proactive approach to help our son by researching what the underlying causes of his pain might be. I talked to many people, learned what foods he should eat, found out how to manage stress, and discovered the ways emotions and energy influenced how effectively he might heal. I was practicing holistic healing, and I didn't even know it at the time!

This book talks about many of the methods I learned to help my son and more: how your energy affects every function of your mind, body, and spirit.

How to recognize the signs when your energy is sluggish, blocked, or excessive; and how to come back to balance with awareness, mindfulness and simple techniques. You will be surprised how easy it is to incorporate and implement these healing practices. Before you know it, you will likely be feeling better, with fewer symptoms and more vitality and well-being.

If you have the sincere desire and the commitment to make positive changes in your life, the knowledge is right here at your fingertips.

It is time to take back your power and be proactive with your physical, emotional, and spiritual well-being NOW! This book accompanies my nine-part online class, **Chakra 101: Know Your Energy**. If you decide to take the accompanying online class, I will be coming to your computer in a five-week period talking about how your chakras function, along with giving you nine homework assignments and offering nine healing meditations.

Please Note: *The information compiled for this book came from my 13,000+ observations since 2006. By all means, this is NOT a Chakra Energy Medicine bible. Your experiences may be completely differently than mine, but within the pages of this book you will gain fundamental knowledge about chakras. I am also planning to write other books going deeper into the topic of chakras.*

To learn more visit www.HealingPlaceEnergySchool.com.

STOP giving away your healing powers! FREEDOM and VIBRANT HEALTH await you, and they are closer than you think. Everything in life comes down to your determination and your commitment to learning the process, and then to make it happen!

Start today. You are so worth it.

Your Energy Medicine Partner,
Helen Chin Lui
Certified Energy Medicine Practioner
Certified Reflexologist
Certified Usui Reiki Master/Teacher

Table of Contents

Introduction

I want to thank and congratulate you for choosing to learn more about your energy. My intention is that *Know Your Chakras: Introduction to Energy Medicine* will give you many useful insights about your inner energy and its flow, as well as help you learn how to be mindful so that you CAN make positive changes in your life in a relatively short amount of time. This book is the beginning of your exploration; by no means does this book contain all the answers.

As a Certified Energy Medicine Practitioner, Certified Reflexologist, and Certified Reiki Master/Teacher with 20+ years of cumulative knowledge, I have directly facilitated and participated in over 13,000 healing sessions. You may feel as though you are supposed to do something, but you probably feel confused and stuck. Let me say you are not crazy for feeling that way. With my background, I can save you time and prevent any self-inflicted suffering from trying the wrong approach. Let this book guide you in the healing of issues and ailments that could be causing you to feel unbalanced and stagnant. It is my passion and my privilege to share my experience and knowledge with you to help you begin the process of feeling more vibrant, healthier, and more balanced in your overall energy flow.

With my knowledge, I decided to establish the Healing Place Energy School LLC to share my journey with you; so you and your loved ones can also find relief to live better and more fulfilling lives. Lessons and online classes are developed for easy understanding and implementation.

Anyone can learn; there are no prerequisites. All you need is have an open mind and a belief and desire that you can heal.

What is Healthy Energy?

Healthy energy is a combination of many aspects that contribute to our well-being. When our needs are met, we are physically, emotionally, mentally, and spiritually happier. We can attract financial abundance, and we are socially engaging. We feel good about ourselves, our energy flows with ease, and we can broadcast our energy in a positive manner. If a life aspect is not being met, it can cause a negative ripple that can dominate our life, leaving us to chase what is missing.

Quantum physics says that we are made of energy, which holds matter together. We live in a world of energy frequencies, and every cell of our body vibrates at a frequency level. Everything influences this frequency-- our thoughts, our actions, and our awareness. When our frequency is flowing at the right speed, we feel the effects immediately.

Unfortunately, modern society pressures us to perform and produce to the point at which we can't keep up with ourselves. Our energy is challenged every day.

Until equipment was developed to read the bio magnetic energy of living organisms (the Superconducting Quantum Interference Device, or SQUID magnetometer), human energy was not considered a component of our health, and there was no way of assessing energy levels. Scientists are now studying how energy healing techniques and spiritual healing methods of Reiki, Therapeutic Touch (TT), Healing Touch (HT) and Reflexology encourage physical, emotional, and spiritual healing.

What Causes Energy Imbalances and Pain?

During the 13,000 healing sessions I have given, I noticed very few people have any understanding of how their body's energy flows. Energy can be balanced, deficient, or excessive; it is rare when it's consistency balanced.

As we go through our day while juggling numerous tasks, over-scheduling commitments, and dealing with the everyday life stressors, your energy can easily get thrown off and become either deficient or excessive. Your body wants balanced energy while insufficient and excessive energy can become the seeds of illnesses and diseases.

Stress is the leading cause of energy breakdown. Everyone possesses a combination of robust and defective DNA genes. Stress can activate those defective DNA genes, and before we know, it can cause a lot of problems for you. I want to share with you how to avoid energy pitfalls and teach you how to keep your energy healthy and flowing consistently.

Most pain comes from suppressed emotions from the past. We address and process pain the way we were taught by our family. Unfortunately, many people do not have the skills to cope and handle sensitive subjects. We end up ignoring our pain with the hope it will go away. Instead, many times these emotions get trapped on our cellular level and become stuck there.

We may not be able to let go of memories, but you can always make a new beginning with the tools that I will talk about in this book. Once you start to understand how to process painful emotions, you can begin to let go of the past with no residual effects.

Can I Substitute this Book's Information for Traditional Medicine?

The answer is **NO**. You still NEED traditional medicine, but you can incorporate a holistic, complementary, or alternative practice into your wellness plan to help to keep your body, mind, and spirit balanced. These straightforward and easy tips can be applied anytime and anywhere. Once you know them, you can incorporate them into your life with ease.

Who Can Benefit from Know Your Energy?

For anyone who is interested in energy healing and has a desire to learn about his or her own energetic system. This is a great introduction to the fundamentals of energy medicine.

Your Roadmap

There are nine powerful lessons in this workbook. Each lesson starts off with an intentional and grounding meditation to help you absorb the information on a soul level. You will find links to these audio meditations at the start of each lesson and at the beginning of every healing meditation. Along with the lessons, there are nine mindfulness exercises to develop your awareness and nine meditations to aid in your healing.

1. Meet Your Chakras?

Discover where chakras are located and what are their individual purposes.

2. Benefits of Having Healthy Chakras?

By understanding how your energy flows, you will be able to adjust your own energy.

3. How Do Your Chakras Affect You Physically, Emotionally and Spiritually?

You will be looking at what are balanced chakras, the causes of imbalance, and what constitutes good energy hygiene.

4. Know Your Seven Chakras

By examining each chakra's traits, you will begin noticing when you feel balanced, excessive, or deficient and learn how to balance your chakras.

5. Learn the Vital Body Parts and Emotions Associated with Your Seven Chakras

You will discover which body parts, organs, and glands are associated with each chakra; what it feels like when they want to do their own thing and make the proper adjustments.

6. Know Your Aura - Your Personal Energy

In this lesson, you will become aware of your personal energy field outside your body and learn how to protect it from negative energy.

7. Power Up Your Chakras

It's crucial to learn how to strengthen your chakras and keep them positive and uplifted.

8. Be Your Chakras' Best Friend

This is all about knowing your boundaries and what you will and won't do energetically that could compromise your integrity.

9. Protect Your Precious Energy Resources

Your last lesson will focus on how to keep your energy strong so tough situations won't overwhelm you and throw you for a loop.

Just think, in nine lessons you can transform your life and support your energy system. You will begin living an authentic and transparent life with integrity.

Please go at the pace that is comfortable for you; this is not a race or a competition.

Your Commitment

You can come back and re-read or listen to the audio meditations whenever you feel like your energy is becoming unbalanced or if you need a refresher. I will also suggest activities, tips, and tools throughout the book to support the lessons. If you have subscribed to the online class, Chakra 101 Know Your Energy, I will periodically add new content and automatically email it to you.

Homework

Most people will not want to do the homework or will merely skim over it, but what they don't realize is that the homework will integrate the energy from this book into your cellular memory for a more profound and lasting transformation. The questions will encourage you to think about where you are in the moment and where you would like to go. Can you do the assignments superficially? Yes, of course, but if you want real transformation, you **have to do the work**. There are no shortcuts.

Meditation Rules

Each healing meditation is about 12-17 minutes long. Yes! Just imagine being with yourself for that amount of time and learning how to let go. I think it's spectacular. Find a place that you won't be disturbed. Tell your family, *"I need this time just to be with me."* Go behind closed doors to your sacred space.

It's vital to shut off all electronics. I know it's hard, but you know what? We can't be connected all of the time to those who think they need us.

Take cleansing breaths. Breathe deeply until your diaphragm moves. I usually take three cleansing breaths. Breathe in through the nose and exhale through the mouth. As I'm breathing in, I'm breathing in positive energy, and as I exhale out of my mouth, I'm letting go of any negative energy that I might have picked up.

Your breath is the most important tool in meditation. This is also true in energy healing and in letting go of any negativity.

It took me almost a year to learn how to be in a quiet space where I could meditate for 45-60 minutes. When you start meditating, your brain will want to talk to you--more chatter than you care to hear. What I still do to this day, when my mind can't quiet down, is say to myself, "Just stop thinking and then come back to quiet."

Sometimes, I repeat this statement 20 or 30 times before my mind completely quiets down. You might have to remind yourself to be quiet 50, or even 100 times.

Don't start to think that you are doing it wrong; just move on and come back to quiet.

Take 5

 Take five minutes and stop to tune in. Listen to the silence behind your swirling daily thoughts and take note.

Journal

It is important to acknowledge your thoughts at the moment by recording any destructive or repetitive thoughts in a journal. Spaces are provided throughout this book to jot down your thoughts. Then allow yourself to drop into your quiet, inner space where those looping thoughts fade into the background, or better yet out of your mind.

A Note on Emotions

Throughout these lessons, emotions *will* come up. Emotions could come from judging our thoughts and then can manifest as a physical ache or pain in the body. Your feelings may run the whole gamut of emotions--from judgment to joy to anger to bitterness. You name it, all emotions will bubble up, especially if this energy has been trapped in your cellular level for a long time. Learn to release it and feel lightness.

Be proactive instead of reactive. Don't wait until you break down to do something about it.

Are you ready to reclaim your power? Let's begin.

Lesson 1:

Meet Your Chakras

I begin all of my lessons with a short and cleansing meditation and to set the intention of what I want to learn. I invite you to do the same. According to Wikipedia, an intention is a mental state that represents a commitment to carrying out an action by planning and having forethought. You create your reality with your intentions and desires.

Listen to the meditation here: http://bit.ly/2ytNRsq

Password: Meet

What Are Chakras and Where Do Chakras Live?

The word "chakra" has a Hindu root and means "disks" or "wheels." All disks and wheels are energy centers. All living creatures have seven energy centers located in the spine from the tailbone to the head. When energy is flowing strongly, the body has the capability of staying healthy, but when the energy is interrupted or blocked, the body can become distressed and imbalanced, which often leads to illnesses.

So just imagine a fuse box in your home. If the electrical circuit is overloaded, it can cause your appliances to stop working due to an interruption or surge in energy flow. It doesn't mean the device is broken; it's just temporarily out of service. It's the same thing for your chakras.

Chakras are your electrical or energy circuits. They are responsible for all of your physical, emotional, and spiritual functions. Once you understand how your energy flows, you can restore power to that part of the body.

For the three years I attended energy school, we had enough time to study the seven main chakras and not the twenty-one minor chakras.

After the three-year program ended, I continued on my own, exploring the major and minor chakras through reading and research. I am still a student of life and will never stop wanting to learn.

The main seven chakras are located in the spine from the tailbone to the top of the head. Minor chakras are located in the hands, arms, legs, and back; each has its own vital and specialized functions.

How do you know if your chakras are in a healthy state? Think about how you feel? Your emotions will dictate how healthy your chakras are. If you feel peaceful, your chakras are flowing with consistent energy flow. If you are in a bad mood, your chakras will fluctuate with either excessive or deficient energy until they come back to balance. Think about when you feel blue, and something doesn't feel right--your chakras aren't happy too.

The Seven Chakras

First or Root Chakra

The **Root Chakra** is located at the groin. It is bright red in color and spins clockwise when healthy.

The **Root Chakra** is about meeting your primary survival needs, such as a having a home, spouse, family, work, food, health, abundance, and joy.

When this chakra is balanced, you feel fantastic and your world is radiating with confidence.

When it is out of balance, fears set in very quickly, which can lead to anxiety about not having enough of your life needs met.

Second or Emotion Chakra

The **Emotion Chakra** is located underneath the belly button; this chakra represents your emotional well-being. It is bright orange and spins clockwise when healthy. This chakra handles how emotions are perceived and processed.

When we feel our emotions, most of us feel on a superficial level. We either feel good or bad about something, but many of us don't really understand WHY we actually feel that way.

To give you a quick example of what superficial joy looks like, let's consider the shoe lover. Shoe lovers are addicted to their shoes. They dream about the next pair of shoes and putting them on their feet. They are ecstatic when they buy shoes, but then, within a short time after the purchase, that happiness and joy begin to fade.

What happened? This was a quick joy fix. There wasn't anything lasting about the emotions other than the chase. Then it is onto the next pair of shoes.

It's the same thing with negative emotions. Negative emotions are emotions that we have unconsciously stored that have not been processed. More often than not, we were taught at a very young age how to ignore and avoid our painful emotions.

What happens with these negative emotions? They slowly amassed while poisoning our thoughts at the same time!

By learning how and why you feel the way you do, is key to keeping all of your chakras in check and balanced.

The goal is not to judge buying the shoes as right or wrong, but to feel the joy that comes because you were able to earn those shoes. View the purchase as an accomplishment instead of feeding an addiction.

When the second chakra is balanced and flowing, so are our emotional responses to life. We neither numb out nor freak out--we simply feel our feelings as they arise and let them move on through.

When the **Second Chakra** is out of alignment we feel anxious or depressed, and our emotional responses are either deadened or heightened.

Third or Self-Esteem Chakra

 Your **Self-Esteem Chakra** is located underneath the rib cage. When healthy, it is bright yellow and spins clockwise. This chakra represents self-esteem, how you feel about yourself, and your sense of control over your own life.

This chakra helps you to stay on track as you coordinate and juggle your many daily responsibilities--family, work, and personal commitments. Our self-esteem is constantly tested by how well we manage and perform various tasks and situations that arise every day. This chakra can often become unbalanced and needs constant monitoring.

When balanced and flowing, the third chakra has us feeling confident, energized, and capable.

When out of balance, our self-esteem suffers, and we become insecure.

Fourth or Heart Chakra

The **Heart Chakra** is about love and is located in the middle of your chest. A healthy **Heart Chakra** spins clockwise and is either green or pink in color.

Loving others is important, but equally as important is the love you have for yourself. I wish more people would adopt the philosophy: *let me take care of myself first before I take care of others.*

The majority of people whom I see at my office almost always put everyone else's needs before theirs, and then they wonder why their hearts, lungs and breasts hurt.

When the **Heart Chakra** is balanced, open, and flowing, we feel love, compassion, and empathy for self and others.

When it is out of balanced we can feel burnout, resentment, frustration, or heartburn; or breast issues can arise.

Fifth or Throat Chakra

The *Throat Chakra* located in the middle of the throat. When healthy it spins clockwise, and is light blue in color.

This chakra is associated with communication and being able to speak your truth. Many of us were taught at a very young age, to keep quiet. How many times have you heard, "You can't say that!"? Many people have learned it is not safe to tell the truth for fear of judgment or other negative repercussions.

It's hard to share and communicate our views without worrying how the information will be received and processed. Most people are trying to figure out how and where they fit into their own lives as they process information. Some people will process information internally and focus on their weaknesses, while worrying how people will perceive them. Then there are others who will take the information and grow from it.

When balanced and flowing, the **Throat Chakra** helps us communicate clearly and effectively.

When out of balance or stuck, we can get sore throats, or earaches; we might feel like we aren't safe to speak our truth for one reason or another.

Sixth or Third Eye Chakra

The **Sixth Chakra** represents the third eye and is located between your eyebrows. The color is dark blue. I call this chakra "*seeing with the inner eyes*." By seeing with your spiritual eyes, you can connect to your intuition. We all have intuitive abilities; it's just a matter of connecting with what you feel and sense.

Because many of us have not been trained to trust our intuition, we give them very little thought and I am amazed how quickly we dismiss our feelings.

When open and flowing; the **Third Eye Chakra** will give us a sense of knowing certain things...they may show up as mini movies or fleeting thoughts or feelings, and our dreams can become especially vivid.

When our third eye is blocked or stagnant, headaches can occur. We can become so caught up in our mundane life that we forget to tune into our intuition and our imagination.

Seventh or Crown Chakra

The **Crown Chakra** is indigo purple in color located on the top of our heads. The **Crown Chakra** is about universal spirituality and not about organized religion.

This chakra connects you to your higher self and the universe's energy.

When open and in harmony, all of life feels united with us and we feel a part of a much bigger picture than just ourselves.

When closed or stuck, we can often feel there is very little meaning or purpose to life and we can become closed to possibilit•• •••••

How Does Energy Flow?

Free-flowing energy will travel north to south (or vice versa from chakra to chakra. The goal is to have all of your chakras open so energy can flow unobstructed.

What Causes Energy to Shut Down and Become Obstructed?

Notice what happens when you begin to feel fearful? For example, let's say you are about to get laid off from work or about to retire, or your children are leaving home--how does this make you feel? Do you begin to feel fear or panic? Do you feel disconnected or displaced? As fears creep into your chakras, they begin to slow down or malfunction. They start to shrink in size and all of a sudden, your energy isn't flowing freely anymore. You start to feel unbalanced, stuck, or blocked.

Note where you feel the blocked energy in your body. Does stomach hurt? Your chest feel tight? Can't use your voice? Does your head hurt?

What Happens to Your Chakras When Blocked?

The energy no longer flows through your chakras. Instead, the energy begins to detour or moves sluggishly around the malfunctioning chakras. Then the disconnected chakras begin to shrink caused by energy starvation.

What Do Chakras Look Like?

Take a look at this healthy person's chakra map. Each chakra has two funnels that meet at the midline of the spine. The front body chakra funnels represent our emotions, and the back body chakra funnels represent our will or our head. The best decisions are made when combining the energy from both the emotions and the will, but most will operate primary from one or the other. This depends on how your energy circuits were

installed at the time of your conception. You might be wondering whether your circuits can be rewired during your life time, and the answer is yes, but it takes work to override your default program.

For example, if you are a heart person, you probably enjoy watching love stories. These stories touch your heart joyfully and filling it with love. Heart people give generously in many ways. They give without attachments, and they sincerely want to make positive impacts. They radiate with positive energy and are voices of inspiration. They are good listeners and people have a tendency to flock to them. Many times, heart people run their energy close to depletion because they give so much of themselves. They are highly reactive in stressful situations and take them time to recover. Heart people need to be aware of how much they give and know their boundaries.

"Heart chakra" dominant characteristics

- Emotional and feel on a very deep level
- Interpersonally dependent
- Wear their hearts on their sleeves
- Very empathetic
- Problem-solving decisions are based on "how it feels" and it may take a while to make changes
- Fairly intuitive and people-pleasers
- Know how make people feel safe
- Need to be part of a community

If you are a person who operates from your will or your head, your personality is geared to making things happen. You are a deep thinker, visionary, or leader. You need to be intellectually challenged and do not seek other people's approval or advice. You go to great lengths to make things happen--to the point it can be a detriment to your emotional health. Will people have a "push square pegs into round holes" mentality. Personally, I am very good at pushing square pegs into round holes.

"Will chakra" dominant characteristics

- More rational and interpersonally independent
- Like intellectual challenges
- Problem-solving decisions made based on "logic" instead of on "how it feels"
- Lives in an individual, autonomous environment and does not need a community
- Do not look to others for approval or advice
- My personal goal is to always be at my mid-point energy range by combining both my heart and will energy. Life is so much richer when we are not force to make decisions at the expense of others or ourselves.

Why are decisions best when made by combining the energy from both the heart and will?

When energy becomes **excessive**, it causes an energy overload and then blows out chakra(s). If the energy becomes **deficient** due to negative emotions, the chakra will shrink and becomes sluggish or blocked. The goal is to keep all chakras as balanced as possible for maximum energy flow.

Correcting Energy Flow

So how do you correct energy flow? A lot of it has to do with being mindful of your thoughts and actions, and monitoring your energy so that it stays consistent. Your energy can fluctuate hundreds or even thousands of times throughout the day depending on how you are affected and respond to various situations. By learning to assess your circumstances, and not over-process what is going on or taking outcomes personally, you can adjust your energy flow—as easily as turning a knob.

Homework

This homework assignment will get you to think about your chakras like friends that you have had for years. How do your chakras serve you? Which ones do you automatically operate from? Which ones are strong and which need strengthening? This lesson will help you to develop your personal energy awareness and demonstrate what you can do to make changes.

Which chakra traits do you identify with?

_____

_____

_____

Which of the chakras do you draw energy from?

_____

_____

_____

Do you live emotionally or willfully?

_____

_____

_____

Which chakras do you consider excessive?

_____

_____

_____

_____

_____

_____

Which chakras do you consider deficient?

_____

_____

_____

Which chakras need balancing?

_____

_____

_____

What changes do you want to make to balance your chakras now?

_____

_____

_____

What is your action plan? (For example: I want to balance my throat chakra, so I will attempt to be more direct and clear in stating my needs and desires)

_____

_____

_____

_____

_____

Notes:

_____

_____

_____

_____

Meet Your Chakra Meditation

This meditation introduces you to your chakras; you will greet them and learn about their functions.

The quick meditation ground rules are:

- Find a quiet place where you won't be disturbed.
- Shut off all electronics.
- Decide if you want to sit up or lie down.
- Quiet your mind if it begins to swirl. Always come back to quiet. You might have to repeat this action 50-100 times until you have trained your brain to quiet down chatter.
- Listen to music, if desired.

Listen to meditation here: http://bit.ly/2BoNN2I

Password: Observation

Take three cleansing breaths, inhaling through the nose and exhaling out of your mouth. You will feel your diaphragm moving when taking full breath. Again, don't judge yourself if you think you are doing this practice wrong. There is no wrong way to meditate. Some will feel more emotions while meditating, while others will feel less or not at all. This is okay regardless.

If you are sitting up, place both feet on the floor and your hands, palms up, one on your lap.

If you are lying down, you may place your hands on your hips. The hardest part of doing a meditation while lying down is not to fall asleep. If this happens, you will hear the meditation on a subconscious level and the healing will occur regardless.

First or Root Chakra

 Place your hands on both hips while taking slow breaths. Breathe in through your nose and exhale out of your mouth as though you are pushing your exhaled breath toward your hands. Now feel the energy of your first chakra, beginning at the front of the

chakra where your hands are placed; then imagine you are feeling the back of the chakra. You are just going to meet and say hello to the first chakra.

Observation:

_____

_____

_____

_____

_____

Take three cleansing breaths.

Second or Emotion Chakra

Place your hands underneath your belly button and feel the energy of the front of the second chakra and then the back. Check in by saying: *hello and how are you today?* Just take not of any impressions you feel. You are NOT judging, just observing. You may write down or record any feelings in your book.

Observation:

_____

_____

_____

Take three cleansing breaths.

Third or Self-Esteem Chakra

Place your hands under your rib cage and feel the energy of the front of the third chakra and then the back. It's amazing how powerful your breathing is, and it can clear all negativity, stagnant energy, and blockages. Check in by saying: *hello and how are you today?* Don't make any judgments about how you feel.

Observation:

_____

_____

Take three cleansing breaths.

Fourth or Heart Chakra

Place your hands on your heart and lungs. Feel the energy of the front of the fourth chakra and then the back. Check in by saying: *hello and how are you today*? Be happy and be in the moment. Just imagine you are meeting up with an old friend whom you haven't seen in a while, and you are genuinely happy.

Observation:

_____

_____

_____

_____

Take three cleansing breaths.

Fifth or Throat Chakra

 If it is difficult to place your hands on your throat chakra (many people do not like having their necks touched), you may leave them in your lap and envision that your hands are gently placed on your throat. Now feel the energy of the front of the chakra and then check in with the back of it. Just say: *hello and how are you doing*? I want you to feel how powerful you are by just being. Again, have no judgment.

Observation:

_____

_____

_____

_____

_____

Take three cleansing breaths.

Sixth or Third Eye Chakra

Again, if it is difficult to place your hands on third eye (between eyebrows) you may leave them in your lap and envision your hands placed on the third eye. This chakra is the center for your intuition, your ability to see with your third eye. Focus your attention here a little longer than usual. Feel the energy of the front and back of this chakra. Can you feel its power? Just say: *hello and how are you doing*?

Observation:

_____

_____

_____

_____

_____

_____

_____

_____

Take three cleansing breaths.

Seventh or Crown Chakra

 Either place or envision placing your hands on top of your head. The **Seventh Chakra** is about your connection to divinity and the universe. It is a powerful chakra that connects your soul to heaven while your feet are anchored to earth. Feel the energy swirling above your head.

Take three cleansing breaths. On the next exhale, you are going to imagine pushing your breath from your crown all the way down to your first chakra.

Continue breathing and sitting quietly until you begin to feel balanced and all your energy circuits are connected once more.

Excellent job! Now you are getting more acquainted with your energy centers and how they operate!

Observations:

_____

_____

_____

_____

_____

_____

_____

Lesson 2:

Benefits of Having Healthy

Chakras

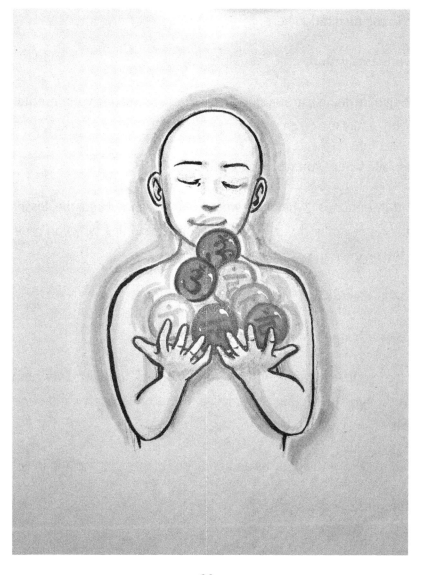

There are so many reasons why we must keep our chakras healthy and flowing. I am going to share what I experience every day in my personal and work life. Please do not let the list below define your experiences; add your thoughts to your journal.

Our focus in this lesson is to begin the freeing process of unleashing ourselves from years of judgment and beliefs that have kept us locked into believing we need to think and act in a regimented manner.

Listen to the meditation here: http://bit.ly/2C9Z03E

Password: Grounding

Let's begin by doing a grounding meditation and setting your intentions for what you would like to get out of the lesson.

Find a place where you won't be disturbed.

Set the intention of what you would like to learn from the lesson, i.e., recognizing negative thought patterns, understanding why you repeat the same lesson over and over again, etc.

Shut off all electronics.

Decide whether you want to sit up or lie down.

Tune into your mind and continue to come back to quiet. Every time you have a thought, just remind yourself that it is unnecessary and come back to quiet.

Continuously take full breaths and feel your diaphragm moving in and out.

Play soft music, if desired.

What are the Benefits of Having Balanced Chakras?

If your seven chakras are healthy, each will rotate clockwise on your spine from the tailbone to the crown. Just imagine a clock placed on your body with its face facing outward, the hands of the clock will be moving to the right. This is clockwise to you.

How do you know when your chakra colors feel bright and alive? The best measuring device is asking yourself how you feel. If you feel upbeat and in a good mood, your chakras are lively and moving. Notice how you feel when you are down or sad. Does your energy feel sluggish and heavy?

When my energy is flowing, I feel a sense of peace and balance. When I feel unbalanced, everyone knows it, because I am not in a good mood. I tend to want to hide from the world for a while to regroup.

Because I am very aware of how energy flows in my body, I can fight off an energy crash before the pain peaks and overwhelms me, causing me to have health or emotional problems. Do you know what causes your energy to crash? For me, my imbalances come from being overworked and stressed.

We can all overcome stressful situations by becoming aware of our feelings. Instead, too many of us ignore our feelings until we begin to spiral down into our dark emotions. By understanding how your emotions operate, you will have the power to interrupt your pain cycle before it accelerates. It is important that you see and handle your daily situations instead of letting those same situations dictate and run your life.

What Do Unhealthy Chakras Look and Feel Like?

First of all, unhealthy chakras stink! They make you feel so uncomfortable and miserable that no one wants to be around you! You don't even want to be around yourself.

Questions to think about:

When you begin to address emotions, how do you process them?

_____

_____

_____

Do you take charge and not let them take you down?

_____

_____

_____

Do you pretend your discomforts don't exist?

_____

_____

_____

Do you go into victim mode?

_____

_____

_____

Do you know if your emotions are coming from you, or are you reacting to a situation?

_____

_____

_____

Do you know what is upsetting or triggering you?

_____

_____

_____

Sometimes we don't even know why we are angry, especially if we have fallen into a habitual cycle where the same scenario repeats over and over again.

Notice where you feel these sensations in your body and their levels of intensity. Do you know what triggers these emotions? How often does the same scenario repeat?

We store our positive and negative experiences on a cellular level. Everyone has the capability to override negative emotions. Like a muscle, your energy constantly needs exercising to build a reserve. Once a reserve has been built, you can manage your energy so that it doesn't fluctuate much and you can come back to balance quickly.

Eighty percent of the people who come to the Healing Place for Reflexology and energy therapy have digestive problems. I know immediately which chakras aren't functioning properly--usually the second chakra for unprocessed emotions and the third chakra for lack of control or self-esteem.

The first step to healing is to become aware of your feeling. **Don't ignore them**. Once you understand your feelings and process them appropriately, you're more likely able to manage and control your energy flow consistently.

Your chakras react to every one of your emotions and are constantly adjusting themselves throughout the day to keep you balanced. If you begin to get emotional, mad, angry, disappointed, etc., your chakras' energy will reflect your emotions by becoming either excessive or deficient.

Your chakras then begin to regulate themselves either by speeding up or slowing down the energy so your chakra can run effectively and smoothly. Again, your chakras are very much like your home electric circuit; they may temporarily shut down to protect you from an energy crash.

You can come back to balance by being mindful of everything you do and say. When I feel like I am beginning to spiral down into my darkness, I stop for two to five minutes and focus on my breathing until my frustrations begin to release. You will be surprise how powerful two minutes of breathing can help to release pent-up negative emotions. During my breathing exercise, I let go of impatience and judgment about the situation and NOT to take it personally. I forgive and meditate to find my peace.

Chakra Vibrancy

Healthy chakras have lively, vibrant color; they spin clockwise; and energy flows from one chakra to another with ease.

Your chakras are always in communication with you. It is a matter of whether you have learned to hear them and follow through on their feedback. Many of us do not trust what we feel, let alone know what to do next. What happens if you do not address these imbalances? Most likely you will feel worse, and this can affect your overall physical and emotional health. It will then take even more time and effort to come back to balance again.

As much as you want change, change can only happen when you are *committed* to making changes. This requires an action plan. No amount of hoping and wishing is going to change anything without commitment and follow-through. (We will talk more how to develop an action plan in Lesson 7 Be Your Chakras' Best Friend.)

Energetic disconnection is an awful place to be. There is usually a feeling of being lost and out of place.

Why Do Chakras Become Unbalanced?

The world of quantum physics states that everything in the universe is made of energy and matter; and all physical atoms are made of vortexes of energy that are always moving, spinning and vibrating. Each one of us has unique energy vortex centers; our biological DNA determines our overall physical health, and our spiritual DNA determines how we look at life.

Our chakras are made of energy vortexes that attract energy and information to us like a magnet. Along with having sluggish and blocked energy, vortex centers can become blocked with negative energy from years of accumulation of stressful situations and psychic debris. Everyone has psychic debris, and no one is exempt from it. Psychic debris comprises of stressful encounters and conflicts with family, friends, and co-workers. How much debris we accumulate depends on how well we have processed our emotions to prevent negativity from building up. Can you let go with ease? Or are you replaying the same painful memories obsessively in your head?

Some Common Energy Issues

Sensitivity and Empathy

Psychic debris is especially problematic for people who are highly sensitive or are empaths. They absorb other people's problems as though they belong to them. They are usually overly involved with family and work problems and tend to take on the archetype of a rescuer or a people-pleaser.

Problem Solver Empaths

Problem solver empaths are NOT ONLY working hard to manage their energy but ALSO managing other people's energy. They become addicted to problem-solving without realizing it.

Worry and Fears

Everyone worries, but if your worries and fears are overwhelming you, these extreme emotions can eventually cause an energy overload or burnout. For example, when a couple has been married for a long time, and one spouse passes away, it is not unusual for the second person to pass soon after. Many say that the widow(er) died of a broken heart. The fear and worry about not living without the other one can take a tremendous toll on the person who is left behind.

Beliefs

What are your beliefs? Our beliefs have been ingrained in us as young children by our parents and community. Most beliefs are passed down from one generation to another without much thought or question. As you become an adult you may start to question your family's beliefs; this can cause a rift in what you believe to be true and causes you to question your beliefs.

Judgments

How and whom do you judge? Is your critical eye getting in the way of your growth? Comparing yourself to and competing with others will stunt your personal growth, because eventually you will reach the point where nothing you do will be good enough. (This is something I am still learning today. What does enough look like to you? And what is good enough?) Often we judge ourselves too harshly if we can't live up to our own expectations.

Learning to be kind to ourselves during this process can be challenging, but it is necessary for personal growth. Be kind to yourself always.

Perspectives

How do you view your world? Do you view your world as half-full or half-empty? Do you live in a positive state of mind? Or do you feel everyone is judging you and you can't catch a break? Instead of looking at circumstances negatively, can you look at what you have achieved and be proud of your accomplishments?

Who is Prone to Unbalanced Chakras?

Modern society is a breeding ground for insurmountable and overwhelming pressure due to rapid changes in both family and work environments. There is so much to figure out--who we are? What are we supposed to do? What are our roles? How do we juggle all of these responsibilities and keep everyone happy? Who is going to keep us happy?

Our relationships with family and work have changed drastically since the last generation. Today's families are more diverse than ever, comprising of a rainbow of different ethnicities, race, and religions. Family units may be blended, headed by a single parent, same-sex parents, or consist of some other arrangement. Some find these relationships mind-boggling and confusing; others accept them with ease.

In the world today, there has been a cultural attitude shift such that we are looking for work/life balance, yet often we still find that we are working harder and longer than we ever have before. We face greater competition to find and keep our jobs, and we struggle to make enough money to support our families. We run to keep up with the competition and new technology. We pray we will not be replaced with lower-cost employees, state-of-the-art technology, or other workplace changes.

Whoa! If these worries don't cause imbalances, I have no idea what would! With awareness, you can ALWAYS adjust your energy level for balance.

When I think of the population who are prone to energy imbalances, these are the people I have met and experienced that immediately come to my mind:

Sensitive empaths – People who absorb and handle everyone's problems like they are their own.

Highly anxious, nervous, depressed people - Their chakras are either excessive or deficient. Excessive energy causes an overload or burnout while deficient energy moves so sluggishly, that it's hard to get motivated.

People who lack boundaries - These people will do everything for others at the expense of themselves. A good example is parents who hover, smother and do everything for their children, not trusting that children can make sensible choices (helicopter parents).

People who are grieving - This is their most vulnerable time.

People who are highly stressed- They can't process their emotions or even organize their thoughts into manageable steps. Stress is made worse by moving from one "busy" project to another without any thought or consideration.

People who worry too much, have too many fears and lack control - Worrying is an energy zapper and can often become a self-fulfilling prophecy when we focus too much on the negativity. We expect and look for adverse outcomes and then attract them to us like a warped kind of magnet.

Those who lack emotional intelligence, or don't know how to connect with others -They often wonder why connections and relationships don't last. They are literally repelling people, and they don't even know they are doing this.

People who have repetitive destructive patterns- Stop If you are beating yourself up! Stop the self-sabotaging behaviors, lack of perseverance, unproductive habits, or feelings of being unworthy. **STOP** and get help. Bad habits are the biggest energy drainages.

Please add your own thoughts to this list and record in your journal.

Thoughts:

_____

_____

_____

_____

To break this cycle, you must establish an action plan that is reasonable and do-able. Did I already say that? Planning is a key factor in making changes that will be beneficial and lasting.

Is It Painful to Open Chakras?

With all energy work, it is best to balance chakras slowly; many emotions can come up at once. For this reason, when you begin to adjust your energy level, it can be overwhelming and even frightening at first. Start slowly and begin by making small changes.

As your energy level changes, your family and friends may start to treat you differently. Why? Your role in their lives will begin to change, too. Two major changes are:

Boundaries

By beginning to establish your boundaries, you'll learn to say "no" or "not now." Your friends and family may need time to get use to not depending on you to fix their problems. You, too, will need time to adjust to your new role of not being the person who puts out the fires or jumps through hoops. Please don't feel guilty if you are not helping.

You have the right not to feel used and depleted.

Views and Attitudes

Your views and attitudes will begin to change, forcing you to evaluate your core beliefs and how they are serving you. Identifying your core beliefs is like solving a mystery of illusions that have been passed down by your family and community. It is best to look at one view at a time and evaluate which ones to keep and which ones you can change and--if need be--let go.

There is FREEDOM in change!

Only you can decide how you want to proceed, please open your chakras at a pace that is comfortable for you. Once open and flowing, find support to help keep them open and to stay balanced. Support can come from a like-minded community, or family and friends who are on the journey with you.

Come Back to Balance

Only YOU can control your balance. Please stop blaming others for your mishaps. It is time to OWN your future.

- Stop chasing things
- Stop thinking that no one loves, hears and supports you.
- Stop thinking that someone else knows more.
- Stop thinking that you have no control or power.

Healing Meditation

Please recognize and acknowledge your strengths. Make time every day to feed your soul. Beware of who and what drains you of your precious energy sources (more about this in Lesson 9). Most importantly, establish an action plan. I can't emphasize this enough. All the wishing and hoping in the world will get you nowhere if you decide NOT to do anything about your situation. This is your choice. Yes, your choice.

Listen to the meditation here: http://bit.ly/2ytHpBC

Password: Healing

Let's do our power-up or power-down chakra meditation. If you're ready, please set aside 20 minutes of quiet time. Shut off all electronics. Tell your family you need some personal time. Your focus is to shut down the chattering squirrel in your head and quiet your mind.

Every time a thought enters your mind, come back to quiet. You may have to do this quieting step 200-300 times during a meditation until your mind and body can quiet itself down. The average person has anywhere from 50,000-70,000 thoughts a day. That's a lot of thoughts!

Your Soul

Your soul is made of spirit and matter. It is created at conception. It is believed it can live many lives. Your soul lives in every aspect of your being. Unfortunately, your soul can become fragmented by exposure to unpleasant or traumatic circumstances. In energy work, the goal is to have healthy and whole (or intact) souls. What does that mean? As we go through the day, we actually leave or give away pieces of our soul without our awareness to everyone we have encountered, like our children, spouse, work colleagues, and friends. Sometimes we give away so much of ourselves that we become spiritually and energetically depleted and incomplete. Calling back your soul is part of knowing and understanding your energy needs.

During the accompanying healing meditation, we will call all of your fragmented soul pieces back to their rightful place in your body. This exercise will make your soul feel complete,whole and peaceful again.

General Meditation Directions

Place your feet on the floor with your hands placed up and open in your lap. You are going to work from your root chakra to your crown chakra.

First or Root Chakra

Place your hands on your hips. Focus on your breathing. Take three cleansing breaths by breathing in deeply and exhaling. Breathe in through your nose and feel the exhaled air move through your chakras until you can feel your breath touch your hands. Your first chakra stores your emotions about having your primal needs met, such as having a home and family, finding fulfilling work, having enough food, and abundance, joy, peace, etc.

Now feel the energy in your root chakra. How does the energy feel? Heavy? Moving? Dense? Does it feel nervous because of unexpected life changes? Or does it feel strong and relaxed because your basic needs are being met?

Whatever you're sensing and feeling, this is what is going on in your root chakra and it is communicating with you.

Energy adjustment – You adjust the speed of your chakras by either breathing quicker or slower. If you find that the energy is excessive, focus on breathing slower by taking full breaths and then exhaling at the same rate.

If you feel your energy is deficient or moving too slow, breathe a little quicker-- but with control so that you don't hyperventilate--and then exhale at the same speed. You may have to focus on this method for several minutes until you get the hang of it and you are breathing in rhythm.

Now do a check in. How does your first chakra feel? You might have to do this breathing exercise two or three times until your energy adjusts or until it is the right amount for you. Keep practicing.

Second or Emotion Chakra

Bring both hands and place them on your second chakra, located underneath your belly button. The same as we did with the first chakra, you may need to do an energy adjustment either by speeding up the energy or slowing it down.

Let's start with a check in first. Take three cleansing breaths. Feel the energy of your chakra increase as you focus on your breathing. Once you have made a connection with your second chakra, now greet it: Hello. How are you? How do you feel? Are you stressed? Do you feel balanced? Is there anything that's bothering you? Can I help you with anything?

See if you notice the little nuances of your energy level. This is a practice that is going to help you to become aware of your body's energy and will help you to come back to balance quicker. Now take two more cleansing breaths.

How does it feel to you? Remember there is no wrong way of doing this. Go as fast or slow as you want. There's no judgment or expectation. Let go of any concerns you may have. Your breath is one of the most important tools in energy work.

Third or Self-Esteem Chakra

Bring both of your hands to the third chakra and place them underneath your ribcage. You're going to focus on your breathing. Take three cleansing breaths. This chakra is about your self-esteem. Your power. Your sense of control. Can you feel good about yourself without judgement? Now check in. What do you feel powerful about? What do you feel you are lacking? Feel this chakra without judgment. Continue focusing on your breath. Breathe in and out two more times.

Check in on how your chakra feels. Have you been feeling low for a long time? Do you have counterproductive thoughts with where you are in life? Can you feel pleased and grateful with what you have achieved?

We look at our achievement in comparison to where we would like to be. Again, it comes back to looking at the glass as half-empty instead of watching it get fuller.

Stop and acknowledge yourself. Give yourself a high-five for being the great person that you are.

Fourth or Heart Chakra

Let's focus on the heart chakra. Place both hands on your heart. I want you to focus on your breath and breathe love into yourself. Remember love is not just about love for your family and friends, but more importantly, the love you have for yourself. It is about coming back to you. You can't give love that you don't have. Start with your soul and feel your own love. Take three cleansing breaths while exhaling and moving the energy from your mouth toward your hands. Feel your heart begin to pulsate with energy.

Stay here for the next minute or two and just connect to your heart. I want you to feel your heart beating just for you. Not for the other people in your life, but for YOU! Come back to the love you have for yourself and feel how powerful you are. If there is too much energy going through your heart, slow it down by breathing slower. Now, take another deep, centering breath.

Fifth or Throat Chakra

Let us now focus on the throat chakra. Bring the energy up into your throat by placing both hands on your throat or visualizing them there. Your intention is to open up your throat so that words can flow from your throat with ease. Ask your soul what words it wants to speak.

Unfortunately, too many of us have been taught to eat our words; this causes the energy to stagnate and can lead to jaw problems, like TMJ (Temporomandibular Joint Disorder), and shoulder issues.

Take three cleansing breaths. Feel for stuck words in your throat I want you to visualize pushing them out. Take a deep breath in and exhale for as long as possible to empty out all the words that have been stuck in your throat. Take two or three more breaths, and each time push out those dead, stuck words.

Sixth or Third Eye Chakra

Let us focus on the third eye chakra located between the eyebrows. This is an important chakra for those who are intuitive or are over-thinkers/over- analyzers. Balancing the energy in the sixth chakra will release imbalances in the head and equalize the energy in the third eye.

You can either place your hands on your third eye or visualize them there.

Now take three cleansing breaths, breathing deeply and exhaling completely through your third eye. Let go of unnecessary and over-analyzing thoughts and judgment that are counterproductive.

Can you feel the unkind thoughts and tension releasing? Keep pushing out negative thoughts while using your breath and exhaling through the third eye. Take two more cleansing breaths. Visualize toxic thoughts being extinguished and vanishing. Do you feel a release?

Seventh or Crown Chakra

 Let us focus on the crown chakra located on top of head. You may either place both hands on top of your head or visualize your hands there. This breathing practice will dissolve unproductive and toxic thoughts that interrupt your connection to the universe, your higher self, and to God.

Take three cleansing breaths. On the last breath, you are going to breathe in and exhale deeply while directing your breath from your crown down to your first chakra. Repeat this process two more times. Just note how you feel after you are done. Keep breathing for another minute or two to completely remove toxic energy debris and connect all the energy electrical circuits in your system. Then breathe this toxic energy completely out of your inner body to your outer body and into your outer energy field, the aura. (See Lesson 6 to learn more about your aura.) You can ask your spirit guides to take away this toxicity. (More about spirit guides and spirit animals in Lesson 5.)

Your Aura

Now radiate the energy from your inner body to your outer body through your breath. Feel the energy radiating out through every pore of your body as it moves into the atmosphere; the universe will take this toxic debris to clean and recycle it. As you continue to breathe out into your aura, visualize wrapping your whole body with your inner energy--like an Egyptian mummy from the top of your head to the bottom of your feet--until you are immersed in an energy cocoon.

Note--how do you feel? Does it feel as though you have removed or released something? You may have to do this exercise several times until you feel everything you want to remove or clear is gone.

Very good!

Do another check in. How do you feel? Lighter? Just stay in this quiet moment for a few minutes. How did you like the meditation? Was it powerful? Did you feel your energy shift during the meditation? Mine did. I always enjoy doing meditations. I always feel so much better afterwards, lighter and more peaceful.

Check in Regularly

It's important to do an entire body and soul check in throughout the day. You don't have to get obsessive, but many people don't know how or when to check in. One thing about toxic debris that it replenishes every day, like tartar building up on teeth; without realizing it, there is so much of it that it requires a tremendous amount of scraping to get rid of it. Negative energy elimination has to be done daily, too. I clean my energy field every night after I get home from work. Your energy wants to support you for your entire life, but you MUST take care of your energy constantly.

Homework

Let's talk about the homework that accompanies this lesson. There is such harmony when our physical, emotional, and spiritual health are in alignment with our energy. Everything goes right. There is a feeling of lightness and peace.

When our chakras are out of alignment, it is frustrating and painful. Whenever I feel off balance, my buttons are easily pushed, causing me a tremendous amount of frustrations. What is worse, as a professional healer, I know and can feel when my energy isn't flowing. I recognize when my energy is leaking out of my body instead of recycling internally. I know I have been unaware, unconscious, and overthinking, and doing way too much.

Before learning extensively about chakra health, I didn't realize that I was energetic hemorrhaging until it was too late and I was crashing energetically often. Sometimes it would take weeks or even months to come back to balance. I am now aware of my energy level most of the time. My best energy depletion indicator is when I begin to have headaches; I know this is a time to STOP. Everyone has bad days including energy healers. I'm quite sure that you have energy leakage indicators too; do you know what they are and do you follow through?

What about those people who have no idea that they have been stuck in a negative energy pattern for years? Not fun!

With the homework, I want you to observe and take note of the status of each of your seven chakras and record how each one feels. Which ones feel secure? Which ones need strengthening? Which ones are blocked or sluggish? By identifying how each one feels, you can begin to correct them.

When I started my journey in the healing arts business in 2006, I was terrified of this change. At the time, very few knew or understood what Reflexology, Reiki, or Chakra Balancing were in the Boston area. I didn't know how I could make a living doing this. Holistic healing was so new that people had no idea how my services would help them; nor did they know what questions to ask. They were more concerned with how much services cost, and whether or not insurance covered the sessions. At no time did they ask how my services could help them. Through the years I have learned to conquer my fears, but I still get nervous when starting new and unfamiliar projects. I now call them "quiet fears" instead of "I am going to throw up fears." Progress can be painful, but it doesn't have to be like that.

How Often Should I Do a Chakra Balancing Meditation?

If you have the time, do a chakra balancing meditation every day or every other day. Once you feel your energy is balanced, you can reduce doing meditations to a couple of times a week, then once a week or occassionally. You will know how much! I do short meditations throughout my day instead one long one. Meditation is easy to do even if you only have a couple of minutes. You can pretty much do a meditation anywhere that is quiet. I also do short 10-second meditations while waiting for the traffic light to change. You will be surprised how helpful and peaceful you can feel afterward even after a 10-second meditation.

By meditating regularly, you will quickly recognize what a valuable tool this is to get your chakras back in alignment.

Thought Provoking Questions

Every question is structured the same for each chakra. I want you to observe each chakra. How does it feel? Heavy, light, sluggish, painful, excessive? Please feel free to describe it as best you can. There is no competition or judgment, no standard of right or wrong. What you feel, will feel very real to you; by accepting your emotions is acknowledging who you are.

Your first chakra is about your home, your family, your spouse, your work environment, your shelter, your food supply, and all of your primary needs.

Do you feel safe and loved in the world?

Your second chakra talks about your emotions. As you connect to yourself, remember your number one priority is "you."

How do you feel about yourself and other people? How have you prioritized your relationships?

Your third chakra is self-esteem, your confidence, and your sense of being in control.

In general, do you like your life?

Your fourth chakra is about your heart. The main character is you. Always come back to you. I know it sounds a little strange to talk about self-love, but if you don't have self-love how are you going to love others?

Do you love? How do you love? How deeply do you love, and can you let yourself be loved?

Your fifth chakra is about your voice, self-expression, and communication with others.

Can you speak freely? Can you speak your truth? Can you do it in a non-threatening way? Can you deliver words that people can hear without using intimidation or judgment?

Your sixth chakra is about your third eye/intuition. We get intuitive hits all the time, but trusting how and what you feel is going to be key in how you will follow through with your own guidance. I follow my inner guidance most of the time; I'm constantly challenging myself to do new things. Am I afraid? Yes, of course, I'm afraid! I've lived in my stretch zone for so long that I have no idea what it feels like to live differently.

Do you trust your instincts and insights?

Your seventh chakra is your crown chakra, your divine connection to your higher self and to God. How do you make that soul connection daily? Come back to discover how good it feels to be in your body and to make that nourishing daily connection. To help find that inner connection, do things that please you and make you happy. Will you continue to have uncomfortable emotions? Yes, you will, but it is okay to feel these emotions, because they are a part of you. Acknowledging them lets you grow from them.

Do you pray or meditate daily? Connect with nature? Look at the sunset or a starry night sky? Can you feel your place in the universe?

As you start to notice and recognize your habits and personal patterns, the choices you make can lead to you to a happy and healthy life. It is the life you are meant to have. Practice with passion what you have learned today.

Observation:

_____

_____

_____

_____

_____

_____

_____

_____

_____

Lesson 3:

How Do Your Chakras Affect You Physically, Emotionally, and Spiritually?

I have worked with thousands of people since the opening of my practice and I have found everybody wants the same life comforts: a joyful and healthy life, a family, a spouse or partner, shelter, food, financial abundance, hope, and peace of mind. All of these wants can be achieved. Absolutely NO ONE is exempt from having their desires met.

During this time, I have worked with only two individuals that have had all their life's comforts met. What have I noticed about their energy? They are confident, don't fret or worry needlessly, eat healthily, move their bodies, have healthy relationships, and don't hold onto their negative thoughts or experiences. I am amazed how they can roll with the punches of life with very little or no drama.

What happens when we fall short of our expectations? We end up spending countless hours fretting and worrying about how we're going to get the things that we think that everyone else has, or wondering why we never got them in the first place.

I can hear you saying, "Yes, I want everything! But how?" A lot has to do with how you manage your energy to stay consistently positive and uplifted. If your mind is in a constant state of processing in a negative thought pattern, think about how difficult and how long it has taken to manifest what you want. If you can be in a high state 80% of the time, you WILL attract beneficial outcomes. And yes, you can still magnetize those things while vibrating positivity at 50%, but it may take longer. Since we live in a human body, I don't believe most of us can be 100% blissful all of the time. It's possible, however, that you might be one of those exceptional people.

What keeps us from getting the life we want? Our negative, unproductive thoughts and fears keep us stewing in our darkness. Unfortunately, like a broken record, these dark thoughts run through our minds regardless of whether we are aware of them or not – then we wonder why we can't catch a break! Without consciously knowing it, you are either broadcasting your wounds and negative vibration OR emanating and radiating vibration from a place of balance and wholeness.

Why We Must Keep Our Chakras Healthy and Vital?

There are so many reasons why we must keep our chakras healthy and vital; in order to keep our bodies healthy, all body systems, hormones, and processes must work in harmony with each other to achieve homeostasis. Good health is achieved through stress management, balanced diet, physical movement, and mindful activities. We must care for our energy in the same manner if we want to keep our chakras and spirit healthy and flowing so that they will give us a lifetime of good health, happiness, and a light soul.

When our chakras (or any aspect of our energy system) are out of balance, it can have a profound impact on our physical, emotional, mental, and spiritual health. We can end up being prone to illness and living an unhappy and chaotic life. If energy is balanced, the feeling of being stuck or blocked can be relinquished quickly instead of lasting for years of needless suffering. If you are in a good place now, continue working on keeping yourself there or grow to your next energetic frequency level from there.

By checking in with each of your chakras daily you can prevent overload and burnout. Once you recognize which of your chakras feels out of place, you can bring them back into balance quickly. Everything starts with awareness and then an action plan. Take notes of how each one feels! And then plan to do something about it.

Some emotions you may feel:

- Strong and powerful
- Joy/happy/pleased/loved/at peace
- Fearful/afraid/bitter/angry/resentful
- Weak/ need strengthening
- Blocked/sluggish/numb
- Too much energy/overwhelmed/flooded

First or Root Chakra

Are you connected and have a spouse/partner, family, home, finances, enough food, work, joy, and peace?

Does this chakra feel light, heavy, sluggish, blocked?

_____

_____

_____

Second or Emotion Chakra

Are you emotionally connected to yourself, and to others?

Does this chakra feel light, joyful, heavy, sluggish, blocked, loved, or unloved?

Notes:

_____

_____

_____

Third or Self-Esteem Chakra

Are you confident? Do you have control in your life?

Does this chakra feel light, heavy, sluggish, blocked, or powerless?

Notes:

_____

_____

_____

_____

_____

Fourth or Heart Chakra

 Do you love yourself and others consistently?

Does this chakra feel loved and light, heavy, blocked, or sluggish?

Notes:

_____

_____

_____

_____

_____

Fifth or Throat Chakra

Can you speak freely and tell your truth?

Does this chakra feel light, heavy, blocked, sluggish, smothering, or fearful of judgment?

Notes:

_____

_____

_____

_____

_____

_____

_____

_____

_____

_____

_____

Sixth or Third Eye Chakra

Do you trust your instincts and have the insights to see ahead?

Does this chakra feel light, blinded, or burdened with too much information?

Notes:

_____

_____

_____

_____

_____

Seventh or Crown Chakra

Do you feel you have a divine connection to your higher self and/or to God?

Does this chakra feel light, dark, sluggish, blocked, or empty? Do you feel a connection with the divine?

Notes:

_____

_____

_____

_____

What changes do you want to make?

_____

_____

_____

Starting when?

_____

_____

_____

What can you do today?

_____

_____

_____

What are your plans for next week?

_____

_____

_____

_____

_____

What would you like to see happen in two weeks?

_____

_____

_____

What about next month?

_____

_____

_____

What can you see happening in six months?

_____

_____

_____

_____

_____

_____

Start small, but make a commitment to take care of yourself. Maybe you'll work toward quitting smoking, making some dietary changes, adding movement into your routine, spending time in nature, or resting more... Or establishing boundaries...Or saying "no" or "not now...Or asking for help...Investing in yourself by going back to school. Put your plans down on paper. Need help? Find an accountability buddy who can help keep you on track. Start a vision board and look at it daily for motivation.

Notes:

_____

_____

_____

_____

_____

Repetitive Dark Thoughts

We all have repetitive dark thoughts that just won't go away, or we can't let them go. Most dark thoughts come from a collection of unresolved painful interactions with family, friends, and work colleagues. How many times have you held back your opinion because you didn't want to start a conflict? Or you were afraid of looking foolish or stupid? Many times, we pretend dark thoughts don't exist until we are forced to review them because someone or a situation has triggered that emotion.

To help break the "stuck" cycle," it is best to recognize what these feelings have done or are doing to you and then decide your course of action. Have these feelings taught you anything or kept you stuck in a cycle? Decide to bring those feelings to closure. The most difficult task is figuring out who and what is bothering you; then having the courage to do something about it. This process takes tremendously amount of time and will probably be painful as you examine layers of pent-up emotions.

Once you recognize your feelings, empowerment begins. Now it is time to develop an action plan. (No change can be made without an action plan. Did I say that again? Sorry.) Please use your journal to write which emotions has owned your life and what you're planning to do about them. Decide which changes you can sincerely make. Don't blow out your action plan into a 15-step healing program and then fail to follow through because it takes too much effort, or you have lost the momentum. Take baby steps that are do-able. Start with the first step. Even acknowledging that a change needs to happen can be your first step.

Take 5

When you begin to have a dark thought, **STOP**. Ask yourself, "Where are these ideas coming from and how are they serving me?" Evaluate whether these thoughts are elevating or draining your energy? By recognizing how your thoughts affect your energy, you can STOP them from escalating, taking hold of your spirit, and sending you spiraling down into dark hole.

Awareness Story

With her permission, let me share a client's awareness story with you. Susan has been coming to the Healing Place for reflexology services since 2011. Her family strongly urged her to seek holistic therapy outside of her traditional medication regimen to manage her rheumatoid arthritis. She finally realized she couldn't control the pain with medication alone. At the time, she described her pain level as a twelve, when a ten is considered the worst for most.

Susan comes every six weeks for a reflexology session; we usually start the session with the same conversation, checking-in on how she feels and if there have been any changes in her condition. On a recent visit in 2017 we had a different conversation. She walked into my office and saw what she thought was a new painting on the wall. "Hey, Helen, do you have a new painting? I don't remember seeing this one." My response was, "Susan that painting has been hanging on the same wall for ten years." Mind you, the picture she is looking at is five feet high and three feet wide and takes up nearly an entire wall in my office. Then, looking at another painting, she says, "How about that painting, is it new?" "Well, no. That has been here for eight years."

What our conversation told me was how unaware she was of her surroundings, of anything other than her pain. She was so much in her head that all of her attention was concentrated on getting RELIEF from her reflexology session--to the point that she couldn't see anything else. I wanted to help her bring her focus beyond just her pain.

Why do we focus on some things and not on others? How do we become laser focused on one thing while ignoring our other needs? Instead of constantly focusing on finding relief for her pain, Susan eventually started to listen to her body and understand its needs. She accepted the fact that there are foods that she can no longer eat because they trigger body inflammation. She decided to make significant life changes by incorporating stress management, regular movement exercises, quality time with her family and friends, and most importantly, quiet time for herself.

As of 2018, Susan manages her pain through diet, movement, healthy relationships, reflexology, and a minimum of medication; her pain level is a one or two instead of a screaming ten.

How Have We Programmed Ourselves to Ignore Signs of Pain?

We all are guilty of ignoring signs of pain; we have learned to override those signals. After a long period of neglect, the mind and body begin to forget how to respond to pain until it becomes unrelenting and ACUTE that we are forced finally to address it.

When we consistently ignore our body's signals--what happens? We no longer live entirely in our body and we lose our connection to it. How often do you ignore your body's signals until it is too late?

This lesson will help you connect to your body, mind, and spirit.

Listen to the mediation here: http://bit.ly/2o2g1e2

Password: Intentions

Let's begin by doing a grounding and cleansing meditation. Set your intentions for what you would like to learn from this lesson.

Don't know what an intention is? According to Wikipedia: *an intention is a mental state that represents a commitment to carry out an action or actions in the future; this requires planning and forethought.*

Find a spot where you won't be disturbed for the next five minutes.

Shut off all electronics.

Decide whether you want to sit up or lie down.

Continue to ease your mind away from unnecessary thoughts. Each time something pops up in your head, say "not now" and come back to quiet.

Consistently take full breaths throughout the meditation as you move your diaphragm in and out.

Play soft music, if desired.

What Are Balanced Chakras?

Let's look at the front and side view of the chakra map. (Please refer to Lesson 1 - What Are Chakras? for their individual descriptions and functions.) Your main chakras are located on the spine from the tailbone to the crown. Notice that each chakra has a front and a back, shaped like a funnel, and they are touching at the points.

For each chakra to be balanced, both funnels must be equal in size and moving in the same direction at the same speed. How will you know if they are balanced? By how you feel! If you feel good, your chakras are balanced. If you feel sad, angry, or disappointed, one or more of your chakras most likely have become unbalanced.

If you can manage your emotions, your chakras will benefit and encourage free-flowing energy. When your thoughts are full of fear and worry, your chakras end up suffering too. They become strained and overworked to maintain their balance.

When energy becomes excessive or deficient, one side of the chakra funnel will expand with too much energy while the opposite funnel will shrink due to the lack of circulating energy. For example, when you are overly excited, and you just can't contain it, your energy circuits become supercharged. Your energy then becomes excessive and moves too quickly, while working to adjust itself until it comes back into balance.

If your energy becomes slow or deficient, your chakras can become sluggish or blocked. Think about how you feel when you receive bad news. What thoughts immediately come up? Do you become fearful and worry? Do you wonder what should you do next? Can't think straight? These emotions negatively are affecting your chakras. In this case, instead of energy circulating throughout your body, your excess energy becomes stuck in your head (sixth and seventh chakras), while your nervous system and adrenals (third chakra) go into overdrive to level off the surplus energy. The remaining chakras then become energy deficient. Notice how you respond in difficult and chaotic situations; this tells you how your response program is wired. If you are unhappy with the way you respond to difficult situations, you can make changes.

You DON'T Have to Live This Way

You can retrain yourself to respond differently. Again, this takes time, awareness, and the desire to change. On a personal note, my chakras are still being tested after 30 years. I know which ones become excessive or deficient and why. How they are triggered and by whom. I hope very much that I will learn how to handle these emotions within my lifetime. Even though I want my discomforts to disappear, unfortunately, it is a learning process. Choose how you want to learn.

When chakras are balanced and open, energy flows from the top of the head to the tailbone and back again. Healthy chakras rotate clockwise and exhibit bright, clean colors. You will most likely feel emotionally happy and healthy when the front (emotion) and back (will) chakras are working in harmony with each other. Once balanced, you can quickly tell when and which chakras are "off," and you can correct them fairly quickly.

Yes, you DO have the power to do this! In fact, everyone has the power to make these changes! It takes awareness and practice, a conscious commitment, and deliberate, focused attention.

How Do We Prevent Physical and Emotional Illnesses? – Energy Hygiene

Unfortunately, very few people know what is proper energy hygiene. Energy hygiene is how you manage your energy flow so that it doesn't become depleted. Your chakras' health is influenced by your lifestyle and how mindful you are. Your energy goes through hundreds and sometimes thousands of daily adjustments to keep you in balance.

Energy health, like your physical health, comprises many daily practices to keep you physically healthy and energetically balanced. These include stress management, knowing your boundaries, and having healthy living habits--eating a balanced diet, moving your body, getting enough rest, and taking time for yourself every day. While these things may seem obvious, implementing them on a consistent basis is difficult, but extremely vital to illness prevention and overall health maintenance.

Many of us tend to live a fairly regimented life with little flexibility and don't notice what affects us until something doesn't feel right and we become overwhelmed. We focus too much on our work, for example, instead of what we need to do for ourselves. You are less likely to listen if your inner critic is always telling you what you are doing wrong or if it takes too much effort to do something about it.

How we individually process our emotions depends on how well we were taught to address our feelings as children.

As children, we want to please and seek approval; we don't question our parents' emotional skills. Very few adults know how to handle their emotions, let alone how to process them. Teaching children how to navigate through emotional upheaval is a skill many people don't have. Many of us have been taught through the generations to ignore our discomfort in hopes that it will just go away; instead, it usually turns into anger, resentment, and bitterness.

Learning how to feel your emotions instead of analyzing them begins the process of healing your body.

Your healing is YOUR responsibility!

What Has Modern Society
Done to Us?

We are moving faster than we ever have while multitasking our lives away. Most of us are stressed and overwhelmed--just trying to get through the day. We live outside of our bodies while losing touch with our inner selves. Let's stop the madness and think about what changes we can make *today*. Learning how to recognize and process feelings and emotions is going to take time. Very few of us want to revisit old wounds, but it is sometimes necessary for real change to come about.

STOP running the same "victim" recording in your head! These thoughts serve no purpose:

- How you got cheated in this life
- How your company laid you off after years of service
- How your children didn't turn out the way you expected
- How your loved one died prematurely or has left you
- How that negative experience is still haunting you after years have passed

Leave these self-destructive thoughts behind. Accept yourself and make friends with your dark thoughts instead of internally fighting them. Breaking the cycle takes consistent, mindful work to stay physically, mentally, and spiritually healthy. Like any workout regimen, you MUST actively work on keeping your spirit healthy.

Emotional Triggers

A trigger is something that sets off a memory or flashback; it can transport your mind back to the time and place when that original traumatic event happened. Emotional triggers can be caused by one experience or by an accumulation of numerous experiences. It can be memories of joy, happiness, judgment, shame, anger, or insecurity.

What are your triggers? Your family? Work? Old lovers? Triggers are very personal, and we all have them. I want to share a story of an incident where one of my triggers was activated while being laid off from a job.

I had been a dedicated employee for years when my company laid me off due to budget cuts. During my time at the company, I had given it my all. I worked hard and dedicated myself to my work to the point that I was depleted and exhausted and had very little energy left for my family.

I put the job ahead of my family. I didn't need to do this, but I believed going beyond the scope of my duties made me a good employee. I learned quickly that this was not the case, and it was NOT GOOD for me or my family!

How did it make me feel when I got the pink slip? Angry, bitter and resentful!

The first thing I thought was that they must have made a mistake. Then I began to wonder if I wasn't good enough anymore. All of this time I had thought I was invaluable and believed I brought value to the company!

Being laid off also triggered childhood memories of when my parents and teachers told me that I wasn't trying hard enough at school and that I wasn't a good student. I tried SO HARD to keep up, and I had very little help to improve my learning skills. My parents were immigrants and knew nothing about the US educational system, but my parents hired a tutor for a short time—until money ran out. Then it was back to learning on my own, and I continued to falter. I was promoted from one grade to the next regardless if I had the skills to move up or not.

Later, as an adult, I discovered I had a learning disability bordering on dyslexia. Those early years were tough for me; I experienced a lot of shame and spent years floundering on my own. I pushed myself to learn by listening to others speak. I read a lot of books and observed different writing and speaking styles. Upon getting laid off, I suddenly was transported back to those feelings of shame: feeling like I would never do or be good enough.

This wound-trigger made being laid off far more stressful for me than it might have been for someone else. After the initial shock of being let go, fear crept in. I was paralyzed by my panicky thoughts:

"How am I going to find another job?" and *"Nobody will hire me because I'm too old."*

I let the fear engulfed me instead of seeing the layoff as a new beginning. Only after the crying and the rage tapered off was I able to calm down and began to look at the situation in a positive way--as an opportunity instead of a tragedy.

Take 5 – Know Your Spirit

What feeds your spirit?

_____

What breaks your spirit?

_____

What are you holding on to? _____

Can you work with your inner critic to make changes?
(Circle One) Yes   No   Not Sure

What do you and your inner critic talk about?

_____

_____

_____

What would you like to change and when?

_____

_____

_____

You must choose a date to begin. Don't wait for the perfect time, because there is no such thing. Waiting for the perfect time is an excuse to keep these changes on the back burner and never accomplishing anything.

_____

_____

_____

Mantras

During this lesson, to reconnect with your spirit, repeat the mantra below until you feel your energy is vibrating differently, i.e., becoming lighter, more peaceful, or releasing an emotion. If you are not familiar with mantras, a mantra can be a word, a sound, or a phrase that is repeated continuously, either in your mind or out loud, to aid in quieting your body and keeping your brain focused on one task at a time. Repeat a mantra as many times needed until the words feel true to you.

Feed My Spirit Mantra

I choose not to live with pain.
I can make friends with my pain.
My life lessons have taught me much.
I am empowered by the knowledge granted to me by my experiences.
I am living with joy and abundance.
My desires are met.

Begin to Process Feelings

When you begin to feel a disconnect from your soul, don't ignore it. These feelings are REAL and they are clues that something is not right with your energy. If you operate from the front of your chakras, your "emotions," you most likely will begin to over-process and over-think the situation and wonder why this is happening to you (like a punishment). If you operate from your "will" chakras, you will most likely become charged up, like a warrior getting ready for battle, and you'll want to fix the problem.

Addressing the cause of your pain is never easy, and it always takes time once you decide you can no longer tolerate your discomfort. It will all become easier with practice. Start with becoming aware of how you feel. The meditation that accompanies this lesson will help you to recognize where your wounds are stored and how to release them. Once you are aware of your emotions, you will recognize signs of anger, disappointment, and failure before they escalate into something overwhelming. These feelings are NOT wrong or bad; they are what make you human. You just need to look at them through a different lens.

I have learned so many things through my misfortunes; I view them as teaching tools to help me to shift to a higher vibration. Why do lessons have to be so hard? They don't have to be, but we have been taught in order earn our reward; it must be earned through hard, painful, and difficult lessons/work. We all believe this on some level. These thoughts turn into emotions that are deeply rooted in our souls--forgotten--until something triggers them. Emotions, like stacked pancakes, fall over when there are too many of them.

Focus on what makes you happy! Like a muscle, your emotional and spiritual connection needs to be worked on consistently until it is toned and infallible.

Your Energy Checklist

When you become emotionally charged and stressed, you are harming your body by depriving it of oxygen. This is especially true when you are energetically charged or if you are hyperventilating. Your sympathetic nervous system goes into the "fight or flight" mode to calm your body by producing three major stress hormones: adrenaline, cortisol, and norepinephrine.

Do yourself a favor and STOP for five minutes and

- Take full breaths, breathing from your diaphragm, until you start to feel better.
- Examine who or what you are angry at. Many times, you are more angry at yourself than the person who you think has caused you the pain.

There is a reason for everything, and nothing is as bad as it looks/seems. (What is the lesson?)

_____

_____

_____

Where do you feel in your body a built-up of energy?

_____

_____

_____

Continue breathing until you feel something releases.

Change Requires Action!

Choose how you want to tailor your life. You can be a victim and blame others for your mishaps. Or you can see every event on your journey as an learning tool and an opportunity to do something different in your life.

For years I had wanted to leave my old job, but I had gotten lazy and complacent; nothing was motivating me to leave. Once I changed my outlook, I no longer viewed being "laid off" as being "not good enough." Instead I chose to use it as a chance to spread my wings and stretch out of my comfort zone. This is when I established my business, the Healing Place in 2006.

Your world is viewed through your perceptions. Perceptions come from what your senses feed into your consciousness. By checking in with your chakras every day you are keeping your energy healthy and your views in-check while paving your way to a happier and more fulfilling life.

Homework

Your homework will help you recognize and acknowledge your feelings so that you can always support good chakra health. By assessing your level of awareness, you can determine what is important to you and have your needs met. Please answer the following questions and record your thoughts. These questions will help you determine where you are at this moment and document your amazing journey as you look back at these entries in the future.

Primal Needs

Rate the importance of each of the following with 1 being the lowest priority and 10 the highest:

Spouse/Family _____   Shelter/Home _____   Food/Water _____
Health _____   Clothing _____   Money _____   Career _____
Other _____

1. Are your primary needs being met? (Circle One) Yes or No

2. What keeps you from having your most important needs met?

Fear? _____ Judgment? _____ Lack of money? _____

Lack of knowledge? _____ Self-esteem? _____

Insecurities?

3. Are you afraid of losing something? Is the situation changing? Yes_____
   No_____ Maybe _____

4. Are you angry, bitter, or resentful that you don't have it? Yes____ No ___

5. What changes are you willing to make to obtain _____?

What is your next step?

_____

_____

_____

_____

Health Needs

Do you have any physical discomfort? If none, skip to the next section.

_____

_____

What are they?

_____

Where are they located?

_____

For how long have you have them?

_____

Has it improved or gotten worse with time?

_____

What scares you the most about your condition?

_____

_____

_____

Are you angry? Bitter? Resentful about your health issue?

_____

_____

_____

Do you view your condition as a punishment?

_____

_____

_____

Do you use your condition as an escape from your everyday life?

_____

_____

_____

Do emotions around your condition consume you?

_____

_____

_____

Do you think your condition is caused by stress?

_____

_____

_____

_____

_____

How does your condition make you feel?

_____

_____

_____

Emotional Needs

What are your everyday needs?

_____

_____

_____

How do you support your needs?

_____

_____

_____

How do you connect to your spirit?

_____

_____

_____

_____

What are your strengths?

_____

_____

_____

What are your challenges?

_____

_____

_____

What changes do you want to make?

_____

_____

_____

1. Are you in a good place in your life? Yes _____ No _____

2. What keeps you from having what is most important to you? Fear? ___
Judgment? _____ Lack of money? _____ Lack of knowledge? ____

3. What are you afraid of losing?

_____

_____

_____

4. Are you afraid of never getting what you want?

_____

_____

_____

5. Is something in your life changing?

6. Is the change(s) making you afraid?

_____

_____

_____

7. Are you angry, bitter, or resentful that you don't have, what?

_____

_____

_____

_____

8. What changes are you willing to make to obtain what you desire?

_____

_____

_____

_____

Spiritual Needs

Rate the importance of each of the following with 1 being the lowest priority and 10 the highest:

Connecting to your soul _____

Connect to Divinity or to God _____

Meditation/Me time _____

Sports/Fitness time _____

Healthy nutrition for a strong healthy body _____

Being consciousness/Mindfulness _____

Other, please name

_____

What is your most important need listed above?

_____

What keeps you from having it? Fear? _____ Judgment? _____
Lack of money? _____ Lack of knowledge? _____

Are you afraid of losing it? _____ Is the situation changing? Yes_____ No _____

Are you angry, bitter or resentful that you don't have it?

_____

_____

_____

What changes are you willing to make?

_____

_____

_____

Of all of these needs, what are you most proud of?

_____

_____

_____

What did you do to attract this energy?

_____

_____

_____

_____

How have you maintained this level of energy?

_____

_____

_____

Power of CHANGE

What changes CAN you make NOW?

- Make a plan.
- Get support.
- Search for knowledge/information.
- Develop the discipline.
- Overcome self-sabotage.

If money and time were no object, what changes would you make today?

_____

_____

_____

Check in with your soul, what is the next step? Baby steps are okay!

- Find courage.
- Look for resources.
- Do the research.
- Get support.
- Get training.

What change are you going to start with?

When?

_____

Where?

_____

Notes:

_____

_____

_____

Healing Meditation

Listen to the meditation here: http://bit.ly/2B0ONar

Password: Greet

This meditation will have you meet and greet your chakras. The goal is to feel the energy of every chakra to see how balanced each one feels. During this meditation emotion(s) may get triggered, but remember, it is only a memory, and it is NOT real.

The steps to prepare for this chakra balancing meditation are the same as the grounding and cleansing meditation at the beginning of the lesson.

Place both feet on the ground (with shoes on or off) and put both hands face up in your lap. Don't clench your hands into fists; this will stop the energy from flowing.

Close your eyes and take three cleansing breaths. With each breath, feel the stress and tension release from your body. Place both hands on each chakra and move up to the next one when cued. Take full breaths through your nose and exhale from your mouth, blowing your exhaled breath down to touch your hands.

All that you will feel and see will come through your senses. Trust what you are feeling as true sensations. Don't doubt what you are feeling.

First or Root Chakra

Place a hand on each hip. Envision your red chakra located in your hip area. Now check in to see in your mind's eye if the chakra is bright red and if it's spinning clockwise at a speed at the right speed. If you feel the energy is moving sluggishly, imagine that you have an energy control knob located on the first chakra. The energy knob is bright blue and glowing. To increase the energy in your first chakra, imagine that you are turning the knob to the right to increase the energy. If the energy is moving too fast, imagine turning the knob to the left to slow it down. Just as you would if you were adjusting a radio frequency, you are adjusting the energy flow through your chakras. You will be surprised how powerful this exercise is.

Take three cleansing breaths to balance.

Second or Emotion Chakra

Bring your hands up and place them on your second chakra, located underneath your belly button. You're going to breathe in and then exhale until you feel the energy move from your mouth and feel the air rush to your hands as you exhale.

You might feel some sensation. Do you see your orange chakra in your mind's eye (your third eye)? A healthy chakra will spin clockwise, and be brightly colored. Notice how the energy feels in your second chakra. If the energy feels like it's moving too fast, then slow it down by turning the energy knob to the left in your mind's eye; if it's too slow, turn the energy knob to the right. Good.

Take three cleansing breaths to balance.

Third or Self-Esteem Chakra

Bring your hands up and place them on your third chakra located underneath your rib cage. You're going to take a breath in and then exhale out of your mouth until you can feel your breath touching your hands. In your mind's eye, note how the energy is moving. Is it spinning clockwise and bright yellow? Does it feel like it's moving too fast or too slow, or does it feel balanced? Now adjust the energy (the right to increase speed and to the left to slow it down) until it is the right amount for you.

Continue to breathe deeply and exhale slowly while your diaphragm moves with each breath. Do not hyperventilate.

Take three cleansing breaths to balance.

Fourth or Heart Chakra

Bring your hands up and place them on your heart chakra or envision them placed there while your hands rest in your lap. Focusing on your breath, you're going to breathe in and then exhale until you feel your breath touching your hands. Can you see your heart in your mind's eye? Is it bright green or pink and spinning clockwise? Let's check in.

Your heart may be full of icky heartache, or it might be incredibly joyful. Whichever one it is, if it doesn't feel balanced to you, adjust the energy either to the right or left until it feels like the energy is the right amount. Can you feel your energy frequency changing?

Keep practicing. You will find the right connection when you can feel your heart become lighter and you feel a release.

Take three cleansing breaths.

Fifth or Throat Chakra

If you are comfortable with hands placed on your throat, place them on your throat; otherwise, imagine your hands are placed on your throat while resting on your lap.

Now breathe in and exhale the air until it touches your hands. Make any necessary energy adjustments either to the right or the left. Notice whether this chakra is spinning clockwise and is light blue.

Many people have problems with their throat chakra due to suppressed words. We are ashamed and embarrassed because of our words. We don't always feel safe when speaking our truth. We are fearful of being judged or saying the wrong things. Forgive yourself for thinking this way. No one is judging you the way you are judging yourself.

I find the throat chakra needs more attention because of how many words we can't express. This energy becomes very stagnant and stuck. Adjust the energy knob either to the right or left until you find the right amount of energy flowing through your throat.

Very good. Take three cleansing breaths.

Sixth or Third Eye Chakra

You may bring up your hands and place them between your eyebrows or keep them in your lap, envisioning them on your third eye--whichever is most comfortable for you. Is your chakra spinning clockwise and bright midnight blue in color? Let's check in with the third eye energy.

The third eye is your intuitive eye. Your ability to see with your third eye depends on how open this chakra is and what kind of thinker you are. If you are an over-thinker or over-analyzer, it can cloud your intuition. Continue breathing and quiet the third eye. Your intuition wants to connect and talk to you.

Now breathe in and exhale out. Every time you exhale, imagine that you are removing accumulated psychic debris from your third eye. Get rid of those unnecessary thoughts that have cluttered your mind.

Take two more breaths.
Check in again and see how your third eye feels.

Seventh or Crown Chakra

Either place both your hands on the top of your head or put them in your lap with palms up. Focus on your breath; you're going to adjust your energy by turning the knob to the right to speed it up or to the left to slow it down. You are going to exhale your breath until it touches your hands. Do you see your chakra spinning clockwise and glowing indigo blue?

Everybody's crown chakra usually moves a little too fast from overthinking. You might need to breathe through this chakra until you feel the dense energy lift.

Take three or four cleansing breaths. Now we are going to move the energy from the crown chakra to the root chakra. Envision moving your energy through a tunnel from the crown to the first chakra. Take a deep breath through your nose, then exhaling the air from the seventh chakra stopping at every chakra, ending at the first chakra.

Continue to take full breaths until you feel all of your circuits are reconnecting and is going back to their rightful places. You may be able to hear this process in your physical ear, though it can be very quiet and subtle.

Your circuits are connecting, one by one.

You did a great job. If you're ready, open your eyes and continue to take full breaths. How do you feel? Lighter? Do you feel as though something has let go? Or do you feel like something is still stuck? If so, do the meditation again. Continue meditating and see what comes to the surface. Note it in your journal.

Please do not judge yourself. Don't worry if you are doing it wrong or be discouraged if nothing came up. People worry what is considered right and take it personally if they do not react in a way that is acceptable to themselves or others. Emotions are so individualized and come with such a range. What may upset my world, you may not think twice about. Any processing, on any level, is acceptable regardless how quickly you go through the process.

Remember, you are already perfect in God's eyes.

Notes:

_____

_____

_____

_____

_____

_____

_____

_____

_____

Lesson 4:

Know Your Seven Chakras

When I was filming this lesson, "Know Your Seven Chakras" for the online class, Chakra 101 Know Your Energy, I was feeling it! I was in a good emotional and spiritual mood. I felt everything was beginning to fall into place, and my feelings told me that my second chakra was juiced and supercharged with positive energy! It felt good to be able to share my knowledge so that everyone CAN and find the FREEDOM to live the life they are meant to live.

Now that you have a basic understanding how chakras can affect you physically, emotionally, and spiritually, it's time to look at the seven main chakras and talk about their purposes and functions. With this lesson, I want to you to be able to recognize when your chakras are balanced, deficient, or excessive, and--most importantly--what you can do to bring them back on track.

Listen to the meditation here: http://bit.ly/2j5hET7

Password: Freedom

Let's start off with a grounding and clearing meditation to set the intention. What do you desire to learn? In order not to have limitations I always say something like, "Whatever I'm meant to learn, I will."

General rules for all meditations are:
- Find a sacred space where you know you won't be disturbed.
- Shut off all electronics.
- Decide whether you want to sit up or lie down.
- Take full breaths through your nose and exhale out your mouth as you feel your diaphragm moving.
- Clear your mind of unnecessary chatter and continuously come back to quiet.

Take three cleansing breaths. Breathe in through your nose and exhale from your mouth as you feel your diaphragm moving. Say to yourself, "I'm ready to learn and absorb whatever information will serve my highest being."

Know Your Seven Chakras

Below is an overview of the general characteristics of each chakra.

First Chakra - Red "Root" Chakra

Located at the base of spine

Purpose – To feel grounded and have all life's primary needs or comforts met (home, partner, family, shelter, food, work, money, health, joy, and peace of mind). Your survival instincts are connected to the first chakra.

When energy is balanced – You feel safe, centered, and at peace.

When energy is excessive – You may be domineering and egoistic, inflexible.

When energy is deficient – You may feel weak or lack one or more of your life comforts and have little interest in material things.

To balance this energy – Move stagnant energy by moving your legs, dancing and swinging your hips, or doing exercises like jumping jacks, running, hiking, walking, jumping, etc.

Second Chakra - Orange "Emotion" Chakra

Located below the navel

Purpose – To feel emotions, be creative, feel desire and pleasure, fertility, and to nurture.

When energy is balanced – You feel good about yourself and others. You are not tormenting yourself with old unresolved emotions or stuck in the "I should" cycle. You can let go of shame and judgment of self.

When energy is excessive – You can be explosive, bossy, and have sexually promiscuous.

If your energy is deficient – You tend to be shy, timid, and frigid. You may lack money, suffer repressed creativity, and experience loss of control.

To balance this energy – Be creative, cook, dance, make a date with yourself or others, do the things that you love to do, and process emotion as comfortably as you can.

Third Chakra - Yellow "Self Esteem" Chakra

Located in the solar plexus directly below the rib cage

Purpose – To recognize your core self, personal power, self-perception, self-esteem, will, and desire.

When energy is balanced – You are cheerful, with high self-respect and a strong sense of self and pride.

When energy is excessive – You are a workaholic and perfectionist, exhibiting manipulative and judgmental behaviors.

When energy is deficient – You have a fear about your identity or losing your identity. You feel invisible or overlooked, are depressed, lack confidence and judgment, cannot take responsibility, and fear failure.

To balance this energy – Massage your belly to move energy. Be honest and kind, be at peace with yourself, do something out of your comfort zone, and take chances.

Fourth Chakra - Green or Pink "Heart" Chakra

Located in the center of the chest

Purpose – To focus your core emotions, including self-love and ability to give love, compassion, harmony, trust, and growth.

When energy is balanced – You are compassionate, empathetic and able to see the good in everyone and everything.

When energy is excessive – You are demanding, depressed, and controlling.

When energy is deficient – You experience paranoia, live in pity-land, are afraid to let go, feel unworthy, withhold love and withhold forgiveness.

To balance this energy – Give freely, do things that make you happy, recognize when you are holding onto something that hasn't served you in years, and start the process of letting go.

Fifth Chakra - Light Blue "Throat" Chakra

Located at the base of throat

Purpose – To facilitate communication and self-expression, making choices without fear or regret.

When energy is balanced – You are a good speaker.

Manifest your desires and live in the present. You have integrity, faith, and self-awareness.

When energy is excessive – You are arrogant, talk too much, (but don't say anything,) attract and create drama.

When energy is deficient – You are timid and can't be heard because lack of voice, or unable to express thoughts, opinions, or emotional needs. Tends to gossip.

To balance this energy – Chant, hum, sing, talk, laugh, or cry to release emotions.

Sixth Chakra — Dark Blue "Third Eye" Chakra

Located between the eyes or eyebrows

Purpose – To harness your intuition, psychic ability, and vision; to reveal how you view your world and have the ability to see truth and wisdom.

When energy is balanced – You accept guidance, have no attachment to outcomes, are free of illusion, and experience a free flow of creativity.

When energy is excessive – You are manipulative, wear a spiritual mask, act overconfident and superior, and overly proud.

When energy is deficient – You lack emotional intelligence (can't emotionally connect with others), overthink, overanalyze, focus too much on the past and most likely not enough on the future, resist sharing the spotlight, and withhold knowledge and wisdom.

To balance – Meditate to clear bad mojo, challenge yourself to go outside of your comfort zone, listen to your inner voice, and follow through.

Seventh Chakra - Violet "Crown" Chakra

Located on top of the head (crown)

Purpose – To maintain a connection with divine spirit and God; to monitor your vision and connection to your soul, intuition, and psychic ability.

When energy is balanced – You accept guidance, have no attachments to outcomes, have trust and faith, and remain connected to family, community, and spiritual world.

When energy is excessive – You are manipulative, arrogant, have a holier-than-thou attitude, and impose your energy on others.

When energy is deficient –You lose connection with yourself, your community, and your spirituality.

To balance – Meditate to balance excessive or deficient energy. Take salt baths to cleanse your aura and realign your body's energy frequency.

Our energy not only comes from the food we eat, but directly from our chakras. We deplete our energy through our daily interactions and our encounters. We can always replenish chakra energy by meditating, expressing our gratitude, with intention, having loving relationships, and being mindful. Our goal is to keep our energy balanced and flowing in the right amount for each of us.

Your Energy Reserves

We withdraw energy from our chakras the same way we withdraw money from a bank ATM. We want to maintain a balance in our bank account. That means we should not withdraw our money to the last penny; NOR should we deplete our energy until it is empty. With a bank account, you may have a backup account for emergency uses, but with energy, there is no reserve unless you maintain one. We MUST always maintain an energy reserve.

For example, if you're a heart chakra person, some of your personality traits include helping others by going above and beyond your boundaries, usually without giving it much thought. You may have a tough time saying "no." Heart chakra people love and want to be needed. You give so much of yourself that you find yourself experiencing energy crashes often and find yourself being too emotional.

How to Replenish Your Energy

Think about what makes you happy and whole, and come back to those practices. Your goal is to strengthen your energy by recycling that energy within yourself so that you don't feel drained or tired. Then you can calm yourself when plagued by excessive energy and also invigorate yourself when your energy becomes depleted. If rescuing others isn't serving your highest purpose, this is the time to learn to say "no, or not now." Give yourself time to determine whether you can sincerely commit to helping someone without regretting it or limit how much help to offer.

Take 5

 To break the pain cycle, you MUST identify and feel your emotions. Then you can process them and decide which ones you can let them go. Look back at the general characteristics of each chakra. Think about which traits you identify with and write them below. Thank these traits for being a part of your life and contributing to what makes you "you."

Reflect upon the following questions in your journal:

Which chakra traits do you identify with?

_____

_____

_____

What physical, emotional, and spiritual feelings are surfacing?

_____

_____

_____

How do they make you feel?

_____

_____

_____

Which of your chakra traits make you happy?

_____

_____

_____

Which of your chakra traits makes you angry, bitter, resentful?

_____

_____

_____

How do you connect with yourself?

_____

_____

_____

Notes:

_____

_____

_____

_____

_____

Healing Meditation

Listen to the meditation here: http://bit.ly/2jVTWt4

Password: Balance

The accompanying meditation will help you balance each of your chakras for health, vitality, and reconnecting with your inner self. You can check in with your chakras anywhere, at any time, and--best of all--no one knows that you are doing so.

The steps to prepare for a chakra balancing meditation are the same as the grounding meditation at the beginning of the lesson.

Place your feet on the floor and your palms, open and facing up, in your lap. Take three cleansing breaths. Breathe in through your nose and exhale through your mouth. Imagine pushing the exhaled air down to the bottom of your feet.

First or Root Chakra

 Place a hand on each hip. Now breathe in through your nose and exhale through your mouth while pushing the air into your hands. Check in with the root chakra and ask: *How are you doing root chakra?* Your chakra will talk to you if you listen. Accept whatever responses you hear. Focus on your breath, and note how the energy feels in the first chakra. Light, heavy, or slow? Now imagine that there is an energy control knob on the first chakra and you can adjust the speed of the energy by turning the knob to the right to speed it up or left to slow it down.

What is your chakra saying? Is it nervous about changes in your life? Or worried about work? Is there something going on with your family? Just observe and don't judge. Just let it be. Talk to your chakra as though you're having a conversation with a friend. Your chakras want to converse and share information with you!

Second or Emotion Chakra

Now place your hand on your second chakra located under your navel.

Take three cleansing breaths and feel the energy of your second chakra.

What do you feel? Are you processing emotions? Is there something going on with you or a family member or friend? Is there a pain you have been avoiding? Just observe and listen.

Are you burdened with other people's problems? Should their problems be yours?

STOP! You are NOT responsible for anyone's emotional garbage but your own! I'm not saying to turn a deaf ear, but you have to define what role can you sincerely play in others' lives. Are you the observer? The compassionate listener? The rescuer? Evaluate whether there is an equal exchange of energy. Do they reciprocate by listening and supporting you when needed? Or do they drain you and walk away when they are done?

Instead of jumping in to fix something, why not empower them with the ability to fix their own problems? Ask them a simple question like, "What are you planning to do to resolve this issue?" This puts the responsibility back on the person who is asking for help. Then, if you choose, to help them to develop an action plan for changes. But don't just fix it for them and be their enabler!

Third or Self Esteem Chakra

Place your hand on your third chakra located under your rib cage.

Take three cleansing breaths.

Feel the energy of your third chakra. How does it feel? Can you feel if it is balanced or not? Are you joyful or are you worried? Focus on what makes you happy instead of worrying or being fearful.

Can you feel the third chakra's energy without having an expectation or attachment to the outcome? Attachments are what get us into trouble when expectations fail us. Do we become disappointed? Can you let go of the negative emotions when you are disappointed?

Take three or more deep breaths to clear out any negativity.

Fourth or Heart Chakra

Place your hands on your heart chakra. Take three cleansing breaths. As you exhale, feel the breaths touching your hands.

Feel your heartbeat. Sense the tender love that you have for yourself and others. You are so incredibly lovable in more ways than you realize. As much as you love others, it's about loving yourself, too.

How can I love myself? Let's dump the shame, judgment, "I should have," and wishy-washy "I think" and feel the butt-kicking power that has always lived within you.

There's nobody like you! You are so incredibly unique. You have gifts–gifts that you are aware of and those that you haven't recognized yet. Continue to focus on self-love and feel the power!

Take three cleansing breaths to balance the energy.

Fifth or Throat Chakra

 Now place your hands gently on your throat chakra or on your shoulders (not everyone likes having their neck touched).

Take three cleansing breaths. Can you see the stuck words in your throat that want to be released? You might be meaning to talk to someone about a concern, but you don't know how to proceed or what to say. Many times, when I can't find the right words, I ask my spirit guides for help, courage, and guidance to find the right words. If you are not familiar with how spirit guides or spirit animals can help you, we will talk more about this subject in lesson 5.

Most of us worry about being judged; we are not comfortable with confrontation, or being seen as a bad person. Believe in your ability to be of service and being able to say what you want to say in a respectful manner.

Take three cleansing breaths to let go of that energy.

Sixth or Third Eye Chakra

Place your hands on your third eye or simply envision your hands placed there.

After taking three cleansing breaths, open your third eye gently to awaken or broaden your intuitive abilities. Envision yourself connecting to either your higher self or to God, spirit guides, or a loved one that has passed on.

What do you see in your mind's eye? Is there something that you want to do? Do you hear a conversation or words? Perhaps you sense or feel something? Do you feel a change is coming to your home, work, health or relationship? Or do you feel content, peaceful and joyful?

Take several full breaths now as you are make your connection to yourself and to God or spirits. Feel that power of intuition in your third eye.

Too many of us do not listen to our inner guidance because we're nervous, afraid, and doubtful of what we might hear.

Your inner self wants a relationship with you. Please listen, and most importantly, follow through on what you hear. Your internal compass is POWERFUL! It will never steer you wrong. The more you follow through with what you feel, your intuition will become stronger and can play a role in your life.

Take three cleansing breaths to release deeply stored energy from your cellular level.

Seventh or Crown Chakra

 Now to meet your crown chakra. You can place both your hands on top of your head, or simply envision placing your hands there.

Take three cleansing breaths. Envision you're making a connection to the universe, God, or, perhaps, to spirit animals. Can you feel a connection to a divine power?

While taking full breaths, imagine pulling that divine energy from the heavens into your crown chakra, then to the third eye, your throat, your heart, your self-esteem, emotions, and then to your root chakra. Do you feel your energy radiating now?

I wish you deep peace and calmness.

Lesson 5:

Vital Organs and Emotions

Associated with

Your Seven Chakras

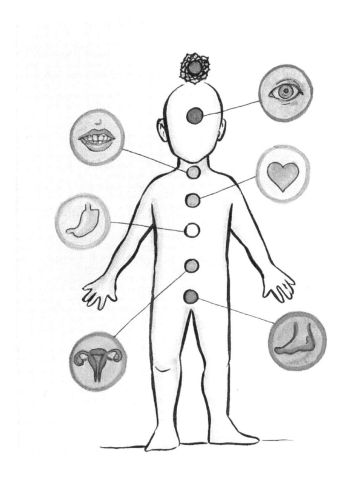

Spirit Guides and Spirit Animals

In the last chapter, I began to talk about spirit guides and spirit animals. If you are a believer in spirit guides or spirit animals, call upon them anytime for support and assistance.

For those who are not familiar with spirit guides, they can either be reincarnated humans, usually loved ones, who have lived an earthly life but have since passed; or they can be dimensional beings from the heavens that have never lived a human life. Their roles are to support and guide us throughout our lives.

In the Native American culture, there is a belief that we are all connected to each other. We are connected to all elements including the moon, the sun, the sky, water, trees, animals, insects, reptiles, fish, etc. Spirit animals come out of this belief of our interconnectedness to the world around us.

How do you know which animals are your spirit animals? Notice what animals you are attracted to or which animal traits you identify with. Do you know why you identify with these particular animals? Most likely you have these animals as part of your animal totem. An animal totem depicts animals and mythological creatures that have spiritual significance to you. The role of spirit animals is the same as spirit guides; they watch and protect us throughout our lives.

We can communicate with both our spirit guides and spirit animals through our five senses: hearing, touch, sight, smell, and taste. We hear them when our bodies are still and quiet. It is difficult to listen to them over loud talk, music, and noise. Meditation is one of the best ways to connect with spirit guides and spirit animals. I hear my spirit guides the best when I am walking my puppies. My tension releases as I focus on my breathing and immerse into my inner sanctuary.

I know my spirit animals are hawks, eagles, owls, and dogs. I am always looking for red-tailed hawks during my walks. I haven't spotted a bald eagle yet in New England, but a few years back, while visiting family in Seattle, WA, I was able to witness six bald eagles competing for fish at a local pond. It was a sight that I will never forget. I am always watching for signs from my spirit animals, and wait patiently to hear their words of wisdom and guidance.

My puppies are my best guides; they tell me when to slow down and take time for myself. Dogs don't get wrapped up in the mundane things that people tend to worry about.

Every chakra has a spirit animal associated with it. Your spirit animals are symbolic representations that will encourage you, help you to find strength, restore balance, and guide you as needed throughout your life.

Grounding and Cleansing Meditation

Listen to the meditation here: http://bit.ly/2o6FH9u

Password: Ready

Declare an intention for what you want to learn. Don't question or limit why you are doing the meditation; set the intention for endlessness. I usually say something like, *"I am ready to absorb this lesson into my soul."*

General rules for meditation are the same as for the previous grounding and cleansing meditation.

Let's examine which body sections, vital organs, and emotions are associated with each of the main seven chakras. You will see how they are tied into your nervous system, endocrine system, and your major glands; and you will learn how to manage their energy levels. At the end of each chakra description there is a mantra for you to recite; the purpose of these mantras is to remove negative energy from your chakras and enforces positive energy flow. A mantra can be a word, a sound, or a phrase that is repeated continuously--either in your mind or out loud--to aid in quieting your mind and keeping your brain focused on one task in the moment. Please repeat mantras as many times as needed until you feel peaceful.

First Chakra - Red "Root" Chakra

Body parts — Base of spine, lower bladder, legs, feet

Possible physical dysfunctions — Chronic lower back, sciatica, leg, and knee pain; rectal tumors/cancers

Possible emotional dysfunctions — Insecurities about life necessities, inability to stand up for self, not being able to provide for self and family

Spiritual dysfunction — Doesn't connect easily with what matters, feel like you don't belong or are not supported

Move stagnant energy — Move your body and stomp your feet. Be in nature and hug a tree.

First Chakra Mantra

I am here.
I am a part of the universe.
I appreciate myself.
I do not lack for anything.
I give and receive with my heart.
I am all that I am.

Second Chakra - Orange "Emotion" Chakra

Body parts — Sex organs, large intestine, upper bladder, vertebrae

Possible physical dysfunctions — Chronic lower back pain, sexual impotency and dysfunction, infertility, urinary problems, candida

Possible emotional dysfunctions – Numbness, feeling lost, loss of control, withholding intimacy

Possible spiritual dysfunctions — Can't connect or identify with others, narcissistic tendencies, lives in isolation

To balance — Learn to enjoy. Accept emotions without attachment and judgment. Learn to focus; limit daydreaming.

Second Chakra Mantra

I am beautiful.
I am alive.
I am whole.
I am joy.
I appreciate my life.
I attract positive outcomes.
I have all that I need.

Third Chakra - Yellow "Self Esteem" Chakra

Body parts — Abdomen, upper intestines, liver, spleen, gallbladder, kidney, adrenal glands, mid-spine

Possible physical dysfunctions — Arthritis, gastro and intestinal problems, liver, gallbladder, spleen, and pancreas problems, anorexia or bulimia; and diabetes   appendicitis

Possible emotional dysfunctions — Self-pity, fear of rejection, excessive need to control self and others, rigidness, fear of failing

Possible spiritual dysfunctions — Regards other people's problems and needs are more important than own, lacks self-confidence, can't eat, feels unworthy, has no sense of belonging

To Balance — Change your self-image. Is it true that you are powerless? Be honest with yourself. Chant and recite mantras often. Learn to release negativity. Believe that you are powerful!

Third Chakra Mantra

I am powerful.
I am seen.
I am respected.
I am heard.
I attract and manifest what I need.
I am unique; I have gifts that no one else has.
I appreciate who I am.

Fourth Chakra - Green or Pink "Heart" Chakra

Body parts – Heart, respiratory and circulatory systems, ribs/breasts, shoulders, arms, diaphragm, thymus gland

Possible physical dysfunctions – Heart problems, respiratory disease, breast cancer, frozen shoulders, tendonitis, and carpal tunnel syndrome

Possible emotional dysfunctions – Feels unlovable, unable to give or receive love, lacks compassion

Spiritual dysfunction – Feels invisible, unable to connect to self, lacks self-awareness, feels unworthy and incapable of love

To Balance – Laugh, watch funny movies, and give freely. Do things that make you happy. Love without restrictions and accept love in return.

Heart Chakra Mantra

I am loved.
I am my own best friend.
I care for myself.
I accept my flaws without judgment or shame.
I am fearless.
I am a super person.

Fifth Chakra - Light Blue "Throat" Chakra

Body Parts —Throat, thyroid, trachea, neck, mouth, teeth, gums, esophagus, parathyroid, hypothalamus

Possible physical dysfunctions — Raspy or high-pitched voice, chronic throat and thyroid problems, swollen glands

Possible emotional dysfunctions — Struggles with one's will, judgmental, critical, gossips, unable to express feelings

Possible spiritual dysfunctions — Low self-value, talks in a small voice, assumes opinion does not count and, therefore, never gives one

To balance — Sing, talk, laugh. Tell jokes and stories. Be like a peacock and show your stuff!

Fifth Chakra Mantra

My words flow with ease.
My words are powerful.
My words are full of wisdom.
My words are expressed at the right time.
My words reduce pain.
I am free of judgment and shame.

Sixth Chakra – Dark Blue "Third Eye" Chakra

Body parts – Brain, nervous system, eyes, ears, nose, endocrine glands (pituitary, pineal, hypothalamus), neurological system

Possible physical dysfunctions – Brain tumor, stroke, neurological disturbances, headaches and migraines, seizures, color blindness, eye problems, ear problems, teeth problems, tinnitus, tiredness

Possible emotional dysfunctions – Over evaluates/analyzes, indecisive, doubtful

Possible spiritual dysfunctions – Shuts down intuition, believes things are too good to be true; so they can' be, feels disconnected with self, believes that everything is someone else's fault

To Balance – Meditate. Follow through with planned actions. Make small changes. Go outside of your comfort zone.

Sixth Chakra Mantra

I am connected to all living things.
I believe in myself.
I trust what I see and feel.
I am knowledgeable and wise.
I am a creator.
I am powerful.

Seventh Chakra - Violet "Crown" Chakra

Body parts – Brain, central nervous system, muscular system, skin

Possible physical dysfunctions – Brain tumor, stroke, neurological disturbances, migraines, memory loss or senility, dizziness, hair loss, seizures

Possible emotional dysfunctions – Over evaluates/overanalyzes, feels disconnected from others, lacks trust, confidence, and faith

Possible spiritual dysfunctions – Shuts down intuition, believes things are too good to be true, fears the unknown, exhibits fear of God

To balance – Meditate. Learn to move energy through the body and feel it. Learn to trust and believe. Listen to your inner voice. Learn to have trust and faith.

Seventh Chakra Mantra

I am a key component of the universe.
I am a part of all living things.
I trust my feelings and thoughts.
I am worthy.
I can manifest my desires
I am powerful beyond my beliefs.

How Your Energy Flows

Your nervous system distributes subtle energy to feed your cells, organs, and body systems. Like electricity that powers up your appliances, your body energy supplies your body's energy circuits.

When energy becomes excessive, your body has gone into crisis mode and has depleted your daily energy allowance. Your body now has to work twice as hard to become balanced again. What causes these energy surges and crashes? Family, work, an unbalanced lifestyle, stress, destructive behaviors, alcohol, leisure drugs, overscheduling--the list goes on.

What happens when energy is deficient? Your cells move sluggishly; instead of staying vital they start to show signs of deterioration. Deterioration can become the seeds for diseases and illnesses.

How to Prevent an Energy Imbalance

Be mindful! Are you aware of your energy circuits and what goes on in your body? If you accumulate stress and don't know how to release it, of if you don't take care of yourself, or you juggle too many tasks, these actions will most likely cause your energy to crash.

To release built up stress, take full breaths throughout the day to release pent-up frustration and find your calm center. You will be surprised how many energy burnouts are preventable by noticing what is going on in your body.

Another way to avoid energy crashes is to learn how to process your emotions. Processing emotions are never simple, but they can transform with the help and support of a professional, family and friends. If you're angry, bitter, resentful, depressed, feeling annoyed, etc. you must acknowledge these emotions. Look closely at what they have taught you? Thank them, and then move on. We spend too much time dwelling on the memories that rob us of our peace and joy.

The goal is to come back to balance again. Choose to STOP living in your discomfort and pain!

Homework

How did you feel as you read this lesson? Did your pain make itself known? Do you know where the pain is located? Stomach? Back? Heart?

Note:

_____

_____

_____

_____

Do you remember when that pain began? Was that time very stressful for you? Perhaps a death of a partner or parent, a divorce, leaving a job, or children leaving home?

Note:

_____

_____

_____

How long did the pain last? Days? Weeks? Months? Years? Is it still with you now?

_____

_____

_____

Physical pain ——The longer you've had physical pain, the more destruction it has caused. You can still heal, but it will probably take more time. Yes, traditional medicine has its place in the process, but it is not always the means to the end. Unfortunately, medication can also be destructive, causing other health problems with detrimental side effects. Please be kind and have patience with yourself during this process.

Emotional and Spiritual Pain —— Along with the physical effects, we must look at the emotional and spiritual disconnect caused by pain. Even though we physically heal, our memories around that pain can linger and still be triggered. We can experience phantom pain for years after we physically recovered. For example, a person who breaks their leg years ago can feel pain when an impending storm approaches. You can say the changing of barometric pressure triggered the pain, but from an energy view, the leg still hasn't healed emotionally and spiritually complete. It as though the leg lives separately from the rest of body and needs individual care. To heal physically, it takes constant awareness and mindful practices to activate all levels of healing.

Take 5

 How many times has a subject come up that you can't discuss because it triggers something that still burns you? Ask yourself honestly, what changes are you willing to make in order to feel better.

How do you know when you have healed? When you no longer feel residual pain associated with that experience, ***then you know it is over***. You have met the pain at a level where you have made peace with it.

This work takes time and patience. Be kind to yourself. Believe that you are doing something even if you're not feeling anything or something is causing you anxiety.

If you still have challenges, then you haven't made peace with the pain yet. Continue to work on this issue by talking to a medical professional, or visiting a professional energy healer, or you can vent by journaling your thoughts.

You must take action if you want CHANGE! Wishing and hoping won't change anything. Waiting to be rescue is a painful process. It takes mindful dedication to make peace with your pain.

Healing Meditation

Your focus during this meditation is to find where your pain lives and quieting it. That sounds scary, and very few people want to look at their pain on an intimate level. However, it is essential that you feel and acknowledge pain. This can be the time to evaluate how the pain has kept you as a victim; with this realization, its time to release the pain. Pain elimination can be simple or complicated, depending on if you are really ready to let it go.

Pain has many layers. The closer you get to the core of the pain, the more painful the process will be, like a severe burn victim that has to continuously clean away layers of dead skin in order for healthy flesh and skin to emerge. Emotionally processing pain is the same as releasing physical pain. Once pain is recognized, you can decide how you want to address it. Depending on how attached you are to the memory, you can either prolong the excruciating process or decide it is TIME to put it to bed. All lessons, good or bad are teaching tools. How you choose to look at the situation and process the emotion are entirely your choice.

During the accompanying meditation, you may only eliminate a thin layer of the pain, and that is all right. The entire process can take a tremendous of time. I have been processing some of my personal pain for twenty-five years, and I am still processing to this day.

There are no timelines or rules for processing. Don't be harsh on yourself if you feel you aren't moving fast enough. No one can determine your successes or failures. Be kind to yourself and get comfortable with the process. If you are not ready to address your pain now, you can put it off, remember, pain DOESN'T go away by wishing, no matter how much you want it to.

Your focus is to locate the pain, thank it for protecting you during difficult times, and tell it to go now because you don't need it anymore.

Listen to the meditation here: http://bit.ly/2j2tQDX
Password: Ease

Find a quiet, undisturbed spot. Set the intention (what you would like to achieve during this meditation). Sit up or lie down. Relax your chattering mind and come back to being quiet.

Take three full cleansing breaths
to begin easing into the meditation.

First or Root Chakra

 To connect to your first chakra, place your hands on your hips and your feet on the floor.

In your mind's eye, you're checking in with the front and back of each (emotion and will) chakra. Check in by greeting each one and listen to their responses. Start with: *Hello, how are you?* Notice what each chakra has to say.

Your chakras want to engage you in conversation. The conversation can be long or short, depending on what they want to say (just like people.) They have been waiting for you to hear them for a long time. Let them talk.

Don't analyze what you hear or feel. The conversation will be similar to the ones you might have with a friend. Everyone wants to be heard, seen, and respected. If you feel any discomfort, acknowledge the chakra and thank it, and wait another time to continue your discussion with it.

Take three cleansing breaths.

Note:

_____

_____

_____

_____

_____

Second or Emotion Chakra

Place your hands on your second chakra located underneath your belly button. Let's look at your emotions.

Feel your emotions - You might be storing a lot of baggage in your second chakra. This consists of unprocessed or incomplete feelings. Incomplete emotions are emotions you began to address but either abandoned when they became too painful or put off because you felt it was not the right time to look at them. Take another cleansing breath.

Feel the emotion. Don't start to overthink or overanalyze what you believe is going on. Don't punish yourself for not addressing them earlier. Just feel it. Ask your chakra what support it needs now.

Take three cleansing breaths. Do you feel a little lighter? Do you feel like something is gone? Note how you feel.

Note:

_____

_____

_____

_____

_____

Third or Self -Esteem Chakra

Place your hands on your third chakra located under your rib cage. This chakra holds your self-esteem, your feelings about your world, and your self-worth.

Take three cleansing breaths. Just feel. What are the biggest frustrations that you've been dealing with? For how long? Does it have something to do with your home, your partner, or your work? What lesson is constantly repeating? Don't judge what you feel. Simply observe.

Note:

_____

_____

_____

_____

_____

Are there lessons you still need to learn?

_____

_____

_____

What changes can you make today? All changes begin with baby steps.

_____

_____

_____

Take three cleansing breaths and
exhale out all destructive energy.

Fourth or Heart Chakra

 Place your hands on your heart. How do you feel about yourself? Feel your energy. You are such an incredible person. What is it that you feel that you don't have enough of? Is this true? Or are your feelings coming from not feeling worthy? See if you can focus on what you have and NOT what you don't have.

You have everything within you--skills, love, and support.

Take three cleansing breaths. How do you feel?

Note:

_____

_____

_____

_____

_____

Fifth or Throat Chakra

Either place your hands on your throat, or imagine your hands are there and place them in your lap.

What words feel like they need to be expressed? Are you afraid to voice your words? Are you scared of being judged? Or sounding foolish?

Focus on your breath and exhale any stored shame and judgment. These destructive emotions can live within you only if you allow them to.

Take three cleansing breaths and move that energy out of your throat. Rid yourself of that negative thought and replace it with something positive. What do you like about yourself? Your situation? Your home?

Note:

_____

_____

_____

_____

_____

_____

_____

_____

Sixth or Third Eye Chakra

 With your hands in your lap or placed on your third eye, focus on the energy of your all-knowing third eye. I call it "my eye behind my eyes," connected to my intuition. Trust what you see. Believe in your truth. Don't dwell on your negative thoughts.

Take three cleansing breaths and feel the power of your third eye.

Note:

_____

_____

_____

_____

_____

_____

_____

_____

_____

_____

_____

Seventh or Crown Chakra

 Focus on the energy of your crown chakra and feel your connection to the universe, God, spirit guides, or spirit animals. Breathe in and exhale slowly until you can feel a subtle energy vibration.

Note:

_____

_____

_____

_____

_____

_____

_____

_____

_____

_____

Now Move the Energy from the Crown to the First Chakra —Take a full breath, breath into your crown, and then exhale your breath down into your first chakra. Continue breathing until you feel a sense of calm.

Can you feel your energy circuits reconnecting and working together? Feel how well your energy is flowing. Your chakras are working in harmony with each other instead of overcompensating.

After this meditation, take a couple of sips of water. Sit quietly, feel your energy, and observe what comes up.

Note:

_____

_____

_____

_____

_____

_____

_____

_____

_____

_____

More Notes:

Lesson 6:

Your Personal Energy Space,

the Aura

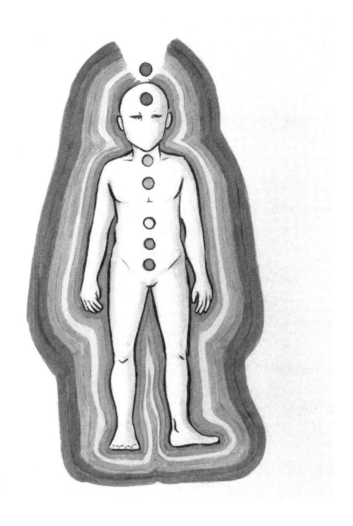

Your chakras are powerful energy generators. Not only do chakras generate and circulate energy within you, but then it radiates out of your body to fill and protect your personal energy space, the aura. An aura surrounds all living and non-living things like a halo. This subtle energy is an extension of your body's electromagnetic field. Your aura contains information about your unique personality, experiences, and emotional and mental characteristics.

The primary function of the aura is to protect your chakras! When your aura is vigorous and whole, it acts as your first line of defense to alert you when something is going awry. Some people call this a *"gut feeling."* With awareness, you can keep your aura healthy by keeping it clean and nurtured; by doing this will also protect your chakras from becoming weak and unbalanced.

In this lesson, you will learn how to recognize when negativity begins to infiltrate your aura and how to prevent that from happening. Healthy auras, like healthy chakras, are the result of positive life experiences, including healthy relationships, good health and emotions and managing your stress.

Before we begin the lesson, let's start with grounding and cleansing meditation, then set the intention to absorb the details of

Listen to meditation here: http://bit.ly/2B1nFYS

Password: Begin

Find a quiet and undisturbed spot.

- Shut off all electronics.
- Take three cleansing breaths and let go of what you don't need.
- You can ask your spirit guides or spirit animals to accompany you on this lesson.
- Decide whether you want to sit up or lie down.
- Quiet your chattering mind.
- Take full breaths through the nose and exhale through the mouth.
- Play music, if desired.

Your Aura - All life forms and non-life forms have auras made of pure energy. The aura encases the entire body in a bubble starting from the top of the head to the bottom of the feet, filling all space in the energy field with energy and light. No two auras are the same. Every aura has its own unique vibrational frequency.

The average person's aura field measures a 10-12" radius around the circumference of the body. The aura can expand or retract depending on how we feel. When joyful and happy, energy can be expanded large enough to fill a room, and when sad and fearful, it can be retracted very close to the body for comfort and protection. Non-life forms, such as rocks, have auras encased very tightly around the object; these auras vibrate with a subtle energy that can neither expand nor retract, and stays a consistent size.

What Causes an Aura to Become Fragmented?

Our auras want to stay healthy and whole, but they can become fragile due to negative emotions resulting from bad habits, conflicts, lack of personal time, lack of boundaries, and destructive behaviors and dysfunctional relationships. These damaging interactions can cause the aura to develop tears and holes within it. Fragmented auras are a gateway to poor physical and emotional health, and spiritual disconnect; they can leave a person feeling physically and emotionally drained and sick.

Everything we do affects our auras. The aura is constantly in a state of change due to vibrational fluctuations caused by how we maintain our physical, emotional, and spiritual states. Even modern-day electronics can affect auras, especially if you are sensitive to the frequencies of radio waves, microwaves, Wi-Fi, and even the planet's magnetic field. We are bombarded by energy frequencies that we don't feel or see but can eventually impact our well-being. It scares me to think how modern society is building "smart homes" with all electronics and appliances connected to Wi-Fi frequencies, while continually exposing us to unnecessary--and possibly harmful--energy frequencies.

Who Can Read Auras?

Everyone can read auras, but most will sense an aura before reading it. For example, if you are meeting someone, can you tell if he or she is in a good or bad mood? If you can, you're picking up on their energy, while feeling and reading the subtle energy being emitted by their auras.

Children and animals can read and feel auras and quickly pick up on moods. Because children's energy is pure, innocent, and unadulterated, they can sense something is feels off, or wrong quicker than adults can. As children begin to lose their innocence, they learn to mimic their parents' responses by watching and learning how to gauge emotional intensity. Animals such as pet dogs instinctively know when something is wrong and begin to feel anxious and restless; they will monitor home activities until the "danger" has passed. Dogs can also sense when their people are not feeling well and will stay by their sides until they feel better. No one taught these skills to either children and dogs; they have a built-in sensory mechanism to alert them when something isn't right.

Activity

Next time you are at the market, pick up two pieces of the same fruit and place one in each hand. Now, notice if you can feel the energy of each fruit and compare them. Can you sense which fruit has a more vibrant energy? Ripened fruit has a higher energy frequency and is likely to be more nourishing than un-ripened fruit that has little or no vibration. When you first start this practice, you may not feel vibration or energy, but with awareness and practice, you will begin to feel the subtle energy of all living things.

Your Aura Knows
Before You Know!

Your aura always knows when something is off before you physically sense it. Imagine millions of sensory feelers touching energy--yours and that of others--while relaying information to you. My feelers are always on. I am always aware of those who enter my energy field while I

constantly protecting my aura from negativity. I do many quick check-ins throughout the day to ensure my aura remains intact and make any necessary energy adjustments. Anytime I feel uncomfortable, or my energy begins to wane, I start my checking in process to see why I feel the way I do. Then I decide what adjustments I need to make.

Aura Alert

The next time you meet someone new, notice how you feel to be in their presence. Are you feeling happy, defensive, or neutral? Perhaps you even feel icky or suspicious. Does meeting this person triggers an emotion or making you uncomfortable? Does your skin begin to tingle and have a crawling feeling? Does your stomach feel like it is in a knot? These feelings are being relayed to you through your aura as it reads the other person's aura. Distressing feelings are early signals that you should protect yourself from the other person's energy.

Consider the Following Situations-

Think about how you react when a salesperson is trying to sell you something you don't want; how does this makes you feel? Nervous? Invaded? Defensive?

_____

_____

_____

_____

_____

When you are in the company of family and friends, whose company do you enjoy? What about them makes you feel this way?

_____

_____

_____

Now notice which people you don't care for and want minimal contact with. Do you know why they ignore you?

_____

_____

_____

I like your vibes moment — When you are in the company of people you like, both your aura and theirs are vibrating at the same frequency and speed. Usually, these events are joyful, and you feel good. Notice how you feel when you are in the company of people whom you don't care for. Chances are good you want little contact with them. Notice how your aura feels. Does it feel tight and close to your body? Are you on guard? Do you feel like you have to protect yourself energetically from the other person because they are saying or doing something that is making you uncomfortable? We are all guilty of taking advantage of other people's energy by nonchalantly engage in non-productive conversation or touching them innocently, and without permission. Can you feel your aura shrinking and looking for quick get away? In this situation your throat chakra is being tested to see if you can use your voice. (More about this subject in Lesson 9 — *How to Protect Your Precious Energy Resources.*)

Déjà vu moment — Your aura not only stores your current life information but also information from your past lives. Think about places you have visited that are new to you but feel as though you have been there before; or remember when you met someone for the first time, but it felt as though you already knew them. These memories are being triggered from your aura's life experience bank.

Psychic moment — Perhaps you are having a psychic moment, such as when you are thinking of an old friend whom you have not spoken to in a while, and then — all of a sudden — the phone rings and they are calling you! You can't explain such occurrences, but your aura is communicating telepathically with the other person's aura while triggering bits and pieces of memories during your awaken and your sleeping hours. As we think and dream about our interactions, desires, and wishes, we are also revisiting our current and past events through our memories, chakras, and auras.

What Do Aura Colors Tell You?

Each aura layer is associated with a corresponding chakra and each has a distinct function. When an aura is out of balance, it needs an energy adjustment like an imbalanced chakra.

Some people (clairvoyants and seers) can detect aura colors. I cannot see colors, but I can see white light radiating from people and objects. I am fascinated with aura colors and love to see the photographs of people who have had their aura pictures taken and the colors interpreted. For those who are interested in aura colors, here is a list and their characteristics:

Red — Enthusiastic and energetic, adventurous, quick to anger, generous with time and energy, possessing a healthy body and mind, direct and to the point

Yellow — Analytical, logical and intelligent, communicates effectively, chooses work over relationships, critical of oneself and others

Pink —Very romantic, loving, and loyal; functions as a healer, highly sensitive to needs, psychic, creative, imaginative, averse to conflict

Green — Highly innovative, strives for perfection and success, stable and balanced, diet-and health-conscious, in tune with nature

Orange — Gregarious, thoughtful, generous, likes and enjoys people pleasing, empathic, quick to anger and to apologize, impulsive

Purple — Loyal and loving, sympathetic to animals, distrustful

Blue — Communicates well, highly intelligent, very intuitive, skilled at organization and motivation, indecisive, workaholic, neglectful of personal relationships

Gold — Loves beauty and art, values friends and community, listens well, generous, seeks to impress

White — Empathic, sensitive, intuitive, adaptable, decisive

Brown — Confused, discouraged, insecure, selfish, can be deceptive

Black — Negative, hateful, sick, depressed

How Your Aura Supports
Your Intuition

Your aura is not only an energetically electromagnetic field that is an extension to your chakras and it is also connected to your intuition. Your intuition is your built-in guidance system that speaks to you through your five senses. Everyone has some level of intuition, whether you know it or not; some call it a *feeling* that you are being compelled to do something without knowing why or how.

We disregard information from our intuition more often than we think because we don't trust the source. Start listening and trusting. The more you follow through with the messages from your intuition, the stronger your intuition becomes, and the more you will believe it, and the more you will follow through.

Intuition Development Practices

Downtime — make time for yourself every day to hear yourself think without judgment and doubt.

Meditation — learn to regroup and collect your thoughts.

Listen — hear your inner voice and then follow through on your guidance.

Create — make and do things that you love. This creates joy.

Music — let the music connect to your soul and raise your vibration.

Practice mindfulness — be aware of what you do and say.

Observe — notice everything, large and small.

Dream — pay attention to your dreams and learn their symbols.

Process your thoughts thoroughly so they don't leave residue—Be aware how you feel.

Find and live your joy everyday!

Yes, it takes work to be mindful! But the freedom you will gain is priceless.

To have strong intuitive skills your aura and chakras must be functioning correctly. Support your energy by committing to keeping your body healthy and active. Get adequate rest. Eat a healthy diet comprised of nutrient-dense foods, move your body to circulate energy, and involve yourself in activities that feed your soul every day.

It is easy to get into a lazy pattern while making excuses that it takes too much effort or you don't have enough time to commit to new practices. Before you know, you're stuck in a negative pattern that you can't break, and you are listening to unsupported voices in your head. Excuses weaken the aura, causing it to develop tears and holes. Instead of energy recycling through the chakras, it begins to hemorrhage out of the body. Weaken energy is the foundation for poor health, negativity, fears, and doubts.

Make a choice, and then stick to it. Do you need help and reminders? There are plenty of phone and computer apps for mindfulness. Food and movement monitors can be downloaded to remind you what, when, and how to create sustainable healthy habits.

Will you fall off the track and lose your way? Most likely YES! You are human, but it doesn't mean you can't pick up where you left off and continue. STOP making excuses! You are worth every minute of your time.

Keep Your Aura Clean and Whole

We are magnetic, energy-charged beings that can detect the slightest energy changes through our nerve impulses. Stimulus signals are transmitted from one nerve to another and create a network of electrical neurotransmitters so that the body can communicate with all internal systems, enabling the body to respond, and react.

Your cells store not only energy for the body's functions but your life experiences too. Feed your soul with uplifting and positive experiences instead of doing the same senseless things daily and causing a buildup of dark and dense energy. Even if you can make one tiny change, you are on your way to building an unlimited energy reserve. Tiny changes are just as powerful as significant changes.

Our energy needs our constant and consistent support. Know your limits by honoring and respecting yourself. Know your boundaries. You are the keeper of your integrity.

Aura Layers and Their Functions

First Aura Layer— Red, associated with the Root chakra; located closest to the body

> *Energy traits* — Connected to the Etheric Body (this is the closest aura layer to the body – root chakra). This layer is associated with your everyday comforts and needs such as home, family, shelter, food, abundance, health, joy, and peace.
>
> *Red personality traits*—Adventurous, generous, enthusiastic, quick to anger, direct, and competitive.

Second Aura Layer —Orange, associated with the Emotion chakra

> *Energy Traits* — Stores your current and past emotions and experiences

> *Orange personality traits* — Connected to emotional, generous, and social. Decisions are based more on feelings rather than logic. Can be temperamental and hotheaded, but quick to forgive. Confident, impatient, and impulsive.

Third Aura Layer —Yellow, associated with the Self-Esteem chakra

> *Energy traits* — Connected to your thoughts, ego, and personal power

> *Yellow personality traits* — Connected to self-esteem and power; analytical, logical, and intelligent; works too hard and focuses on getting tasks done, Can be overly critical. Prefers own company to a gathering and doesn't follow the crowd.

Fourth Aura Layer —Pink or green, associated with the Heart chakra

> *Energy traits* — Able to love and connect to self, to others, and to God

> *Pink personality traits* — Speaks and lives from the heart. Draws people in, admires beautiful things. Highly creative and works hard. Strives for perfection. Down-to-earth. Loves the outdoors, health conscious, active.

Fifth Aura Layer — Light blue, associated with the Throat chakra

> *Energy traits* — Ability to communicate and pursue truth

> Light blue personality traits — Communicator, potent speaker and writer. Truthful, serene, and highly intuitive. Acts as a peacemaker. Can take on too much and feels overburdened.

Sixth Aura Layer — Dark blue, associated with the Third Eye chakra

> *Energy traits* — Consciousness, unconditional love, and intuition

> *Dark blue personality traits* – Divine spiritual devotion. Loyal, and can be traditional. May have problems with balancing emotional and logical responses. Very driven to follow desires. Passionate and opinionated.

Seventh Aura Layer - Indigo violet or purple, associated with the Crown chakra

> *Energy traits* - One with the universe and the divine

> *Indigo Violet traits* - Spiritually connected. Exhibits a sense of knowing and oneness. Works toward enlightenment. Aware of life purpose. Sees the big picture.

Where Do Our Emotions
Come From?

Most of our emotions come from our conditioned beliefs. These beliefs were taught to us as children by our parents and most likely have been passed from generation to generation without much explanation. We believe our family's beliefs blindly. We spend our lives convinced that these beliefs are real and genuine, but what happens when we begin to evaluate their validity when they no longer serve us anymore?

Some examples of conditioned beliefs are:

- *We must work hard in order to be successful.*
- *Laziness breeds more laziness.*
- *You must provide for your family.*
- *Independent thinking is dangerous.*
- *In order to be whole, you must marry and have children.*
- *Don't question the wisdom of elders, teachers, and doctors.*

There are thousands, perhaps millions of beliefs shaped by your background and culture. Think about what beliefs your family taught you. How have they shaped your views? Are you passing these beliefs on to your children? Have these beliefs caused conflicts within you? Have you begun to challenge them? Are they creating fears and turmoil? What if you did everything right, but things still didn't turn out the way you hoped? Are you disappointed? Have you failed? You may wonder why you can't attract what you are looking for. All of these emotions can cause energy disruption and disturbances in the chakras' and aura's energy flow while disconnecting you from your soul.

Homework

The homework will help you to develop your energy muscles so that you can manage your overall energy flow to prevent energy crashes and depletion. Enter all responses in your journal. Remember there are no wrong answers; all responses are correct, even if you can't answer the question.

Are you aware of your aura? Yes_____   No_____   Somewhat_____

Are you sensitive to other people's energy? Yes_____   No_____ Somewhat_____

Can you read, sense, or feel other people's energy?

_____

Do you absorb other people's energy and take on their emotions?

_____

_____

_____

Does your intuition alert you when something doesn't feel right? Yes_____   No_____   Somewhat _____

What are those events? _____

_____

_____

What does your aura alert you about the most?

People

_____

Situations

_____

Danger

_____

Something is about to happen

_____

*Other*_____ _____

_____

_____

_____

_____

_____

_____

Which of your senses does the alert come through?

Smell

_____

Touch

_____

Feel

_____

Taste

_____

Audio

_____

Do you follow through with what you feel? Yes____   No____
Sometimes____

Are you easily overwhelmed by energy and emotions? If yes, in what types of situations?

_____

_____

_____

What are your strongest energy personality traits?

_____

_____

_____

What traits would you like to strengthen?

_____

_____

_____

What would you like to change now?

_____

_____

_____

Notes:

_____

_____

_____

_____

_____

Lesson 6: Your Personal Energy Space: *Know Your Chakras*
the Aura

Feel Your Aura Meditation

Listen to the meditation here: http://bit.ly/2o8qi8q

The rules are the same as for the grounding and cleansing meditation at the beginning of the lesson.

The goal of this meditation is to ask your aura questions and feel its energy layers. Whatever emotions come up during the meditation reflect your true feelings. Don't be afraid of your emotions overwhelming you. Feel them as though you are watching a heartfelt movie. Acknowledge your emotions and then thank them for shaping who you are. If it is possible, listen to your emotions without judgment, bitterness, or shame.

Feel your aura in two steps:

Push the energy out and away from your body - We will begin by moving our body's molecules. Start by vigorously rubbing your hands together for one minute. Place both hands on your belly. Continue to breathe in and out. Feel the warmth of your hands. Now note your hands tingling against your belly. Continue to breathe in and exhale, moving your hands slowly away from your belly directly in front of you, moving them through the seven layers of the aura. Notice how long you can feel the energy between your belly and hands. What does this energy feel like? Warm? Slow? Energetic? Nothing?

Push the energy back towards your belly - Take another cleansing breath. Slowly bring your hands toward your belly as though you are pulling the energy back. Notice how the energy feels. Fuller? More concentrated? Take another breath and as you exhale, push the breath against your hands. Do you notice the energy is changing its intensity?

Are you ready to feel your aura? You may feel some of the layers better than others. Keep practicing. You will eventually make a connection with every layer.

Let's feel each of the seven layer of the aura, one at a time. Anytime your hands have cooled down, *rub them vigorously again until you can feel the molecules moving*. Then place your again against your belly while connecting to the energy there.

First or Root Layer — Take a breath, and push your hands out two or three inches away from your belly to feel the first layer of the aura. Notice the energy between your hands and your belly and what it feels like. If you have any questions about your home, family, work, abundance, spouse, etc., this is the time to ask quietly or out loud. Whatever you feel or whatever response you get, note it and honor it.

Second or Emotional Layer — Bring your hand out another two or three inches, and notice if the energy is changing. Take another breath, and exhale out toward your hands. Can you feel the energy is changing and becoming more intense? Do you have questions about your emotions? This is a good time to ask yourself. Be honest.

Third or Self Esteem Layer — Bring your hands out another two to three inches, and notice the energy. Breathe in, and exhale towards your hands. Note how you feel. Do you feel secure about your future? Do you have the confidence to go forward? What are your doubts? Are they real or are you only worrying? What are these feelings attached to?

Fourth or Heart Layer — Bring your hand out another two to three inches and feel your heart. Do you feel stuck energy in this layer? Ask yourself sincere questions about your relationships and where you are with them. There might be relationships that should have ended a long time ago, but you hold them to them because they are comforting.

Continue to bring your hands out further away from you for each layer up to the seventh layer; ask yourself questions and be prepared to hear some hardcore and sometimes, painful responses. Your answers are authentic reflections of your soul. Your soul wants to guide and support you in your life purpose efforts, but you have to listen and act accordingly.

Once you have observed all seven layers of your aura, it is time to push the energy back towards your body slowly and feels its intensity.

Notice how some of the layers feel more intense, while others feel empty. If you feel that some of the layers need more energy, continue to breathe into that layer until you can feel the energetic vibration changing. That layer may require more love, power, or even acknowledgment.

Practice feeling your aura until you begin to feel a shift. Remember there is no wrong way of feeling your aura. Just observe and see what comes up. The most difficult part of energy healing is not to put your interpretation into what you feel or what is going on. Just be open.

Today, and everyday, treat yourself with kindness and love.

Notes:

___

Lesson 7:

Power Up Your Chakras!

Energy Flow

Energy! We need energy like we need oxygen! It keeps us healthy and vital. It powers up our lives with definite physical, emotional, and spiritual zest. Without healthy energy flow, it is easy to feel empty, depressed, and powerless--as though our life plug has been pulled. By keeping our chakras healthy, we can have an endless surplus of energy and able to override any destructive thoughts, behaviors, and patterns that come our way.

Too many of us have forgotten or never knew how to manage our energy while living in a world of stress, with nonstop swirling demands and having too little time. We often wonder how we are going to get through the day while conditioning ourselves to override the feelings of discomforts until something breaks.

This lesson talks about how you can proactively seek all that you want by building powerful chakras for super energy flow. Everyone can increase their life force energy by removing obstacles and understanding their energy flows. Once you know how to unleash your energetic superpower, you will find balance and peace, have long-lasting and meaningful relationships, act as the creator of your universe, achieve your personal and financial goals, and enjoy an endless supply of energy.

Both the homework and meditation that accompany this lesson will feed and power up your chakras in simple and easy ways. You can incorporate these tips any time, even if you only have a few minutes.

As always, let's start off with grounding and cleansing meditation so that you can absorb what you need to from the lesson.

Listen to the meditation here: http://bit.ly/2Ap2qzl

Password: Present

General Meditation Rules

- Find a quiet and undisturbed spot.
- Shut off all electronics.
- Take three cleansing breaths and let go of what you don't need.
- Set the learning intention.
- Quiet down your mind.
- Ask your spirit guides or spirit animal to assist and accompany you in this lesson.
- Play music, if desired.

Be Energy Positive!

Powering up your chakras comes from living a full life with awareness-- being present, positive and uplifted. Will you have times when you feel down? Yes, of course--after all, we are humans! We all live with some level of anxiety caused by uncertainties, fears, and doubts. Many times these emotions are temporary, and they will pass. By addressing them as soon as possible, they will NOT overtake us. For those deep-rooted, emotions that have been with us for a long time, it is going to take time to look at them and understand why they have such power over us. I want to be honest; personal processing work is NOT easy. It is going to take time with plenty of slip backs. As mentioned in previous lessons, no one wants to revisit old wounds, but it is a necessary step to healing. By building your energy muscles from the inner core, this will give you sustaining strength to overcome difficult situations.

People often ask me to explain what is the difference between feelings and emotions. Your emotions are hardwired into your DNA. Emotions comprise a variety of physical and cognitive responses that you will automatically activate without thinking. For instance, if you sense danger, you will most likely hide or get away until you feel safe. Fear is a universal emotion that everyone experiences, though what triggers it may be more individual from person to person.

Feelings, on the other hand, are very personal associations and reactions to what we sense, feel or perceive. Feelings are individual, collected through our life experiences. No two people will interpret a feeling or see a situation the same way as another.

Being aware of how you *feel* is the first step toward being mindful. Everyone has a level of mindfulness. The more you can consciously tap into your feelings and evaluate your surroundings; the more profound your mindfulness will become.

Mindfulness is a state of being present with your thoughts, feelings, bodily sensations, and your environment. Some people are more aware than others, but the super-aware, empathic people, can sense and feel with an acuteness that can be very painful and emotionally turbulent to them. Volatile emotions can be a way of life for them and are very overwhelming. Like any skill, emotions can be managed with awareness and practice.

Mindful Practices

Here are my top 10 daily mindful practices which I practice most of them daily. My list may differ from yours. Please create your list and DON'T compare your list to anyone's else. This is not a competition!

- Instead of becoming fixated on one solution– look at my options. This is where most of us get stuck when we don't know what to do next. Don't get anxious. Go into your quiet and review choices.

- Strive for a balanced lifestyle comprising of family, friends, and work. If I can't do everything in one day, I don't beat myself up about what I didn't get to. Instead, I focus on my top two or three tasks. The other tasks were not that high priority. Only I can define my balanced scale.

- Eat a healthy diet. A healthy diet translates into healthy energy.

- Monitor my stress levels and do something to defuse it before it drains me. My clue to stop is when my body is tired or when my puppies summon me to walk them.

- Listen to my body when it tells me to STOP and rest. This is my most challenging task for me due to my high productivity level.

- Don't overextend or over-commit, even when I want to do more. Respect my limits.

- Spend a minimum of an hour daily moving my body for energy and to support my bodily functions.

- Connect daily to my spirit by visiting with the universe, my spirit guides and spirit animals.

- Find "me or quiet" time daily. Make time to do NOTHING, even if it feels like laziness or a waste of time. Quiet times are essential for everyone's mental health.

Be your own best friend!

PositivePeople

Positive people radiate high vibration frequency, and their energy feels like a magnet. Everyone wants to be around them. They help others to see the good in themselves and are supportive of the task at hand. Positive people love to give, and they tend to give way too much of themselves. As a result, many are left emotionally drained and depleted. Learning boundaries are especially important for these people.

What do we love about positive people?

1. They find and see the best in situations and people.
2. They radiate happiness.
3. They care for themselves so that they can be their best.
4. They are perpetual cheerleaders.
5. They see the glass beyond half-full.

Why Do We Have Negative Thoughts?

Negative thoughts are usually deeply rooted and embedded on our cellular level while continuously replaying in the background. Just like a dandelion with deep roots that sprout again and again. No matter how many times the plant is pulled up, it keeps regrowing. Negative thoughts work the same way as dandelion roots; they wait for the right moment to come to the forefront of your mind to cause heartache, anxiety and other emotional issues.

Negative thoughts impact every aspect of your being. Once you start to think negatively, these thoughts begin to weave its destructive energy into every molecule of your body. Negativity is so powerful that it can:

1. Stops you from achieving what you want to do
2. Leads you to questioning your self-value and self-worth
3. Lowers your self-esteem
4. Robs you of your joy
5. Drains your energy
6. Replaces your kind thoughts with degrading, fearful, and doubtful ones

How Do Negative Thoughts Begin?

Our identity is connected to our family's beliefs and values. Many times we are taught harmful energy habits without realizing how destructive they can be. Think about how many times your family talks about the same painful circumstances and relives that same pain repeatedly. Most pain patterns are generational, becoming part of the family's model for interaction. Have you noticed how often your family engages in negative talk and what fuels the dialogue?

I would like to share a personal experience. While I neither gossip nor do I engage in trash talk, my family, on the other hand, enjoy gossiping. They treat gossiping like a hobby. (Sound familiar? One day while attending a family event, my mother said something uncomplimentary about a family member. Without thinking, I agreed with what she said. Within seconds, I knew I made a mistake. Once I sided with her, she felt I gave her permission to tell everyone about that person's mishaps. Then the rest of the family began to chime in and voice their opinions. Like a wildfire, the conversation got out of control and lasted longer than it needed to. I learned a valuable lesson that day--do not participate in trash talking, nor agree to gossip or start a fire.

How is Negative Energy Stored?

Who has planted destructive thoughts in your head? Your parents, elders, teachers, church leaders, and friends? Like any recording, if you hear the same thing often enough, it becomes a part of your thought process. If expressing yourself as a child wasn't an option in your family, unresolved emotions begin to stack up over time until we feel numb, unhealthy, depressed and anxious. Our relationships then feel strained and unfulfilled. The negative thoughts that have been with us the longest are usually the most difficult to let go because they are so deeply rooted into our beings.

The more you understand where these feelings are coming from, you will know how to build your energy muscles to overcome them. Eventually, you will begin to appreciate, understand and accept who you are without judgment and shame. It will become harder for negative emotions to take root and overwhelm you. By learning how useless these negative thoughts are, you WON'T allow them to take you down into a spiraling darkness.

What Are Your Unconscious Habits?

Are you aware of your thought patterns? Most of us don't have a clue. When emotions come up, do you know where they are coming from and why? Your brain stores thoughts and your body then stores the emotions associated with the thoughts. For example, whenever you feel anxious, where in your body do you feel the emotion? Your stomach? Your chest? Or in your jaw? There is no emotion that does not affect your body, regardless if you are aware of it or not.

Most thoughts are habitual and have a definite pattern, but it doesn't mean you cannot reprogram how to respond. By becoming aware how you react, you can decide to behave differently and make the needed changes. We have gotten used to ignoring and then swallowing our emotions that we no longer can process them. Hurt feelings do not go away; they wait to pop up when triggered.

The next time a conflict arises and triggers a memory, notice if it is the same lesson repeating? Ask yourself what it is that you still need to learn from this situation? Don't hide from the problem, all you are doing is adding to your ever-increasing stack of unresolved emotions.

How did your family shape your beliefs? Were your parents supportive, or were they always telling you that you were too sensitive, or that your thoughts and feelings were wrong? Did they dismiss your feelings? Were you plagued by self-doubt, always questioning your beliefs and worth? All too often, beliefs are passed down on automatically, without any rationale, other than "this is how we have always done it."

Let me share with you some of my family's beliefs. My mother believes that there are ONLY three ingredients for a successful and happy life and no one should deviate from this life recipe. She worked hard on selling us her version of a "perfect life" and reiterated over and over how "having it all" would bring us happiness and security.

My mother's life recipe is:
- Get a good job that make a lot of money.
- Get married and have children.
- Eat well for good health.

But what happens if you don't have a great job or make a lot of money? Does this mean you have failed? What if you don't want to married or have children? Does this mean you've failed? What if you can't afford to eat healthfully? Does this also mean you have failed? Is this is all there is to life? What about the other life ingredients, such as joy, peace, or laughter? I was one of those kids who asked a lot of questions. My questions challenged my mother's beliefs. Even now, I can see the frustration on her face every time I asked her something that she can't answer. My mother still wonders, *"where did I come from?"* What my mother was conveying to me, unconsciously, were her own fears of being hungry, alone, penniless, and homeless, which she has experienced in her lifetime as a war survivor.

Even though my mother has achieved her three successful life ingredients, she is still unhappy and lonely. She thought by programming her children to "live the American Dream" this would provide her a lifetime of happiness, security, and companionship. Unfortunately, this has not been the case. She has never grown beyond her life recipe, instead of living a full life, she is stuck in "survivor mode." I feel sad that my mom will never see life's beauty.

What are your beliefs? How have they defined you? Success for one person may be different than for someone else. You can change your life to reflect your individuality and not your tribal's beliefs.

Make your own life recipe. Your ingredients can change many times during your life time until you find the right one for you.

What Causes Energy Imbalances?

We are creatures of habit, following the same general routine every day. We meet our obligations first, before taking care of ourselves. Through living a mundane, robotic, and regimented life, most of us have forgotten who we are. We lack understanding of what our true needs are and what factors cause our internal struggles. Our energy flow is continuously teetering between positive and negative.

The imbalance of positive and negative energy is the fundamental cause of human suffering because it steers us away from living in a state of harmony with ourselves and our surroundings. Controlling our environment has become our primary focus, and understanding ourselves has become secondary.

Our thinking process is done with very little awareness when we are dwelling on our anger, resentment, and bitterness instead. These feelings can be devastating when our essential needs have not met. Over time, these emotions begin to poison us with negativity and are the most difficult to process and release.

There are many ways we throw our energy off balance, and most are self-inflicted.

Ask yourself:
- If you are the giver in the relationship, what happens if the giving isn't reciprocated? How does that make you feel? Do you feel like you are being taking advantage of? Most givers love to give because it makes them feel good and they continue to give until they are depleted.
- Are you the anchor in your relationships?
- Do people depend on you for constant help or rescuing?
- Do you recognize when you are giving too much?
- Do you believe everything that is said about you?
- Do you believe what you tell yourself?
- Do you judge yourself and others ?
- Do you believe it is your fault?
- Do you deserve to have nice things
- Are you overworking to avoid living your life?

If you answered YES to any of these questions, they are FALSE beliefs. They restrict your growth. These beliefs are not worthy of your time or energy. Each statement is an energy drainer. Choose to STOP feeling like this and reverse the thought by replacing negative thoughts with positive affirmations. Anytime you think negatively, train yourself by asking "*is this true?*" Most likely it is not. The mind can exaggerate any situation by making it look worse than what it is. These thoughts serve no purpose other than to keep you dwelling on your negativity.

Where Do Your Emotions Go When Tested?

Most emotions are triggered by past events, family, work situations, or friends. In my case, my darker thoughts and feelings are triggered by my mother. We are two very different people. My mother's archetypal energy personality is "poor me and victim." Even though she has lived in America since 1953, she has chosen not to learn to read or write in English due to her fears of being judged on her ability to communicate effectively. She obsessively worries that she isn't able to have her needs, even though her needs have always been met. Instead of living life, my mom waits for the next disaster to strike. My family and I work to help her to control her anxiety attacks, but it only takes the smallest of things to trigger her panic button.

Many of my mother's emotions were shaped during her childhood in China when her family fought for their survival during the Sino-Japanese invasion of 1937-1945. During those war years, she and her family ran and hid caves to protect themselves from the Japanese invaders. Many of her fears from those years still live within her, similar to symptoms of Post-Traumatic Stress Disorder (PTSD). She lives in a constant state of anxiety and can be easily triggered when her routine is disrupted. She worries about running out of staples, even though she has the privileges of having ample amount of food, a roof over her head, and stability for decades. Because her fears are so deeply embedded within her, it is impossible to override her current energetic program for positive flow. Unfortunately, she has never learned coping skills to manage her fears even though the desire is there. It has become easier for her to live with her fearful emotions than addressing them.

How have YOU been tested? Dealing with my mom's fears has been a challenge that I had to overcome so that I wouldn't get dragged into her negativity. Has rescuing taken a toll on your spirit? How does it make you feel? Do you enjoy being of service, or are you resentful? It takes a tremendous amount of energy to help those with emotional needs. If you recognize that rescuing no longer serves your highest good, it may be time to evaluate your relationships and establish firm and clear boundaries.

Your Boundaries

Without clingy or draining toxic energy, who would you be? Your inner gauge will show you how well you can live within your boundaries. You will know if you are helping people or enabling them. As you grow energetically stronger, you will recognize when people are depleting your energy sources instead of feeding it. Most likely you will begin to pull away from these people to protect yourself, or they will fall away because they can no longer feed off your energy.

Every day you must take extra care to replenish your spirit and soul by doing things that you enjoy doing to keep yourself grounded and peaceful.

Positive Thoughts Right at You!

You CAN activate your happiness, health, and success by believing you deserve everything you want! You CAN and WILL attract positive outcomes; this is *the law of attraction*. What you put out there WILL come back to you. But you must sincerely believe, without a shadow of a doubt, that you deserve it; otherwise a grain of doubt will cancel positive outcomes. Put what you want out there! Believe that-

- You deserve all that you desire.
- Visualize the life you want and work towards it.
- Have a positive attitude and think positive thoughts.
- Get up in the morning and get dressed for the day, regardless of whether you have somewhere to go.
- Fake it, until you make it.
- Don't let anyone sway you from your path.
- Be grateful for all that you have.

Success takes time and work. What works for one person may not work for someone else. You are the only one that can define success for yourself. To get there, it takes RESILIENCE, COMMITMENT and ACTION!

Desire, Consistency and Physical Stamina!

Do you have these attributes to make changes? If your boundaries are defined, will you have the discipline required to maintain them? What is the most significant cause of not getting what you want? DOUBT, FEAR, and SELF WORTH. You will NOT receive what you believe you shouldn't have. Choose to see yourself differently.

Are your needs being met?

- Are you meeting and supporting your needs?
- As much as we want to control the outcome of every situation, that is impossible.
- Be tolerant of conflicts. Managing the emotion around conflict is difficult especially if our needs are not acknowledged.
- Learn to listen and communicate your needs effectively is a powerful skill to have.
- Be flexible with your timetable.
- Let go of your ego. You don't have to be right all of the time, and you don't have to win every battle.

You will succeed if you have a positive attitude, maintain good habits, set goals, be flexible, and make good choices. There will be days when you just don't feel like making an effort or have made mistakes. Keep working on your goals and something will grow from your efforts.

Keep moving forward!

How Does Negative Energy Affect Our Emotions?

Modern society is saturated with negative emotions. Our lives are busier than ever. We are assaulted with 24-7 information and notifications vying for our attention. It is difficult to figure out what we need to know, what to respond to, and what to ignore. Added to that is the continuous threat of job elimination, job loss, and company downsizing while balancing work with families and personal time. No wonder we are exhausted.

We are bombarded with stress and negativity. It's everywhere. Everyone has something to complain about or to be skeptical about. Instead of absorbing negativity, you can bullet proof your aura and your chakras from being energetic bombarded.

Take 5

 The next time when you ask a common question, such as "How are you?" Notice how the person respond? Most will automatically answer without thought--"Good," or "Nothing to complain about." Then I ask, "It sounds like you do have something to complain about?" The responder suddenly becomes aware of what was said and wonders why he or she answered without thought. By asking this one simple question, this will help the person to increase their awareness.

We are surrounded by many layers of negativity that it is difficult to maintain optimism. As we live in an increasingly growing electronic world, our face-to-face interactions have been replaced by social media, emailing, and texting. Electronic communication has robbed us of in-person interactions and prevents us from building a community; while leaving us feeling lonely, isolated, and chronically stressed. Think about how has electronic communication affected your quality of life?

To break a negative cycle, you MUST go outside of your comfort zone and do something different.

Start off with being honest with yourself and determine if you have had enough of your current situation and what realistic changes can you make. Remember it doesn't have to be a big change, but you have to begin somewhere and do SOMETHING different today!

One of my favorite expressions is:

Insanity is doing the same thing over-and-over again
and expecting different results.

How Many Times Have You Repeated the Same Lesson?

When we resist learning our life's lessons, we sabotage our growth with excuses like, "I'm not ready," "I don't want to do the work," and "There is too much to do." We are telling ourselves that we are not worth the time or the effort, and that it is easier to suffer than to make changes.

What happens next? The lesson tends to repeat over and over again until we finally understand what we are supposed to learn.

Take more than 5

1. What lesson have you resist learning? How many times have you repeated the same lesson with different people and different circumstances? Notice if it is the SAME lesson with different players and new places.

2. How does it affect your energy?

3. What would you like to see different?

Every time you encounter a repeating scenario, this is a sign of unconscious resistance. You can accept or postpone a lesson; but the lesson will not go away and it will always call you until you are ready to learn it.

If you can open your mind to change, regardless of how painful it may be, the reward can be very fulfilling. If you resist change, you will always be stuck in an energy cycle of "*I wish, I could have, would have and should have and why didn't I?*" These sabotaging emotions will fill your heart with pain while blocking your chance to move forward.

Stop feeling and acting like a victim. No one owes you anything. Everyone feels like a victim occasionally, but when you can't break the victim mentality, it is time to get help! I'm not saying breaking the cycle is easy, especially for those who have had horrific experiences, but only you can decide your starting point. Something has to motivate you from deep within to take the next step.

Breaking Out of the Victim Cycle Requires Awareness and Taking Action

Here are some action steps:

Own it — Recognize the lesson and own it instead of blaming others. or your circumstances.

Take responsibility — What am I going to do next? This is an empowerment statement!

Be grateful for everything you have learned — Please don't tell yourself, "It could be worse." Why would you want to attract negative outcomes to yourself?

Forgive Yourself — Don't belittle yourself for every wrong thing you did.

STOP! — And be still!

Reflect — Know who you are! Define your boundaries by knowing what you will do and what you won't do.

Love yourself and give yourself a break — If we fall off the trail one day, get back on; no one is stopping you from continuing with your journey.

BE GRATEFUL for everything.

How Does Negative Energy Affect Your Spirit?

Positive energy attracts positive outcomes, while negative energy disconnects you from your spirit and soul and weakens your aura. Negativity can become a way of life, and it can be easily rationalized. We are all taught to mistrust from an early age, often hearing expressions like, *"If something is too good, then it can't be real,"* or *"That person is being too good to me-- they must want something or are trying to take advantage of me."* If your perspective on life is negative, you are conditioned to believe in Murphy's Law *"Whatever can go wrong, will go wrong, and whatever can go right, will probably go wrong, too."*

These beliefs keep you living a fear-based life where the odds of your taking chances are slim. It also prevents you from living your life's purpose while keeping your spirit small and living in darkness. You will never fully radiate your beautiful light.

Break the Negativity Cycle NOW!

Start by acknowledging your emotions instead of pretending they don't exist. Take ownership of your feelings. It takes practice and dedication to make a change, to see the world through the lens of "what can go right" instead of "what can go wrong." With practice and awareness, you will recognize when you speak and act out of fear and doubt. Challenge yourself to find the courage to make a change.

When you begin to overcome your conditioning and your limited beliefs, you will realize and see your CHOICES! You will have control over your circumstances, and you can CONSCIOUSLY design the life you want. Believe you deserve more and BREAK the victim cycle. You are the ONLY one who can make life changes. No amount of support from family or friends can help you if you are too afraid to challenge yourself. If you were a friend, what advice would you give to yourself?

Gratitude, gratitude, and more gratitude.

Homework

We all have good and also not-so-great days. When we are in a good mood, our days feel light, happy, and empowered. When we have lousy days, we are moody and grouchy, and we become a magnet for negativity.

Bad Day?

Everyone is allowed to have bad days! It is normal. No one can be "on" 24-7; nor are we built to be "on" all of the time. If you have days when you feel off, this is a signal for you to take care to replenish your soul's energy source. Do things that give you joy and peace. Unfortunately, society encourages us to overdo and over schedule, while running on empty is expected and accepted behavior. Energy depletion takes a toll on everyone, causing us to have frequent energy crashes. We then don't have the energy to sustain ourselves throughout the day, and it can take a long time to feel balanced once more.

Signs of an Energy Crash

Fatigue-

- Feeling disconnected from oneself
- Feeling drained or having no energy
- Feeling sick, without any clear cause.

Recognize the signs of energy crashes before negativity strikes. Do self-care practices every day for balance, strength, and power. Once such practices are adopted, it becomes easier to stay balanced and powerful.

The questions below will help you to focus and take the steps you need to care for your physical, emotional, and spiritual bodies. You can sprinkle these practices throughout your day. Start by being aware of what you do and say. Make a plan if you know you are going to be in a difficult situation. Don't become attached to the outcome and have an open mind. Do you need help to figure out the next step? Ask someone you trust, a professional, or an energy medicine practitioner.

What stresses do you want to reduce?

_____

_____

_____

What do you do for quiet or "me" time?

_____

_____

_____

How do you want people to treat you?

_____

_____

_____

Can you say "no, thank you" or "not now" to family, friends and work?

_____

_____

_____

How do you feed your body? What is your favorite foods?

_____

_____

_____

What do you want to eliminate from your life?

_____

_____

_____

How do you move your body and for how long?

_____

_____

_____

_____

_____

_____

Do you give gratitude to yourself and to the Divine?

_____

_____

_____

There are many ways you can replenish energy, and it doesn't take a lot of time. You will be surprised how helpful even five minutes of peace can be. Plan to do something for yourself every day. Energy crashes are very painful, sometimes lasting days or weeks. Be preventive instead reactive!

- Find quiet time by meditating, chanting, or singing.
- Get out in nature.
- Move your body through any type of movement.
- Eat foods that don't weigh you down.
- Breathe fully from your diaphragm.
- Declutter and get rid of things that you haven't use in ages.
- Unplug from your electronics for a period of time.
- Write in your journal to free yourself from frustrations.

Please do not judge yourself or feel bad if you are not on track one day, start again the next day. There is no getting it wrong in this evolving process. Just keep moving ahead and don't look back. This is NOT a competition!

It is all about YOU!

Healing Meditation

This meditation is to feel how powerful you and your chakras are and appreciate each chakra individually. Let go of any perceived thoughts.

Listen to the meditation here: http://bit.ly/2ArASZV

Password: Connect

The meditation rules are the same as the grounding and cleansing meditation at the beginning of the lesson.

- Place your feet on the floor, and your opened hands on your hips.
- Take three breaths, inhaling through your nose and exhaling from your mouth while pushing the exhaled air toward your hands.

First or Root Chakra

 Connect to your first chakra and feel the energy. What does it feel like? Does it feel balanced? Excessive? Deficient? Correct the speed of the energy by breathing into it. Imagine that you are turning an energy control knob to the right to turn up the energy or to the left to slow it down. Acknowlege what you feel while slowly taking three breaths.

Second or Emotion Chakra

 Bring both hands up and place them on your second chakra, located underneath your belly button. This chakra is not as small as you think it is.

Take three cleansing breaths and return to balance by either turning the knob to the right for more energy or turning it to the left for less energy. Acknowledge what you feel while slowly taking three breaths.

Third or Self-Esteem Chakra

Bring your hands up and place them underneath your rib cage; focus on your breathing. Take three cleansing breaths to balance by increasing the energy or slowing it down. Acknowledge what you feel while slowly taking three more breaths.

Fourth or Heart Chakra

Bring your hands up and place them upon your heart chakra. Your hands will cover your heart, breasts, and lungs. Slowly take three cleansing breaths and release what needs releasing. Either adjust the energy to the right for more energy or to the left for less.

Acknowledge what you feel while slowly taking three more breaths.

Fifth or Throat Chakra

Bring up your hands and place them upon your throat chakra, or envision placing your hands on the fifth chakra while your hands are placed in your lap. Now focus on balancing the energy either by increasing the energy or slowing it down. Let go of any words that do not serve you. Acknowledge what you feel.

Take three slow cleansing breaths and acknowledge what you feel.

Sixth or Third Eye Chakra

Bring your hands up and place them upon your third eye chakra, between your eye brows or place your hands on your lap. By setting your intention, you can balance the energy in your third eye without placing your hands directly on the third eye (or any chakra). Check in with the power and bring it back to balance by increasing or decreasing the energy in the third eye.

Take three slow, cleansing breaths and acknowledge what you feel.

Seventh or Crown Chakra

Place both hands on your crown, or envision setting your hands on top of your head while your hands rest in your lap. Take three slow, cleansing breaths, inhaling energy while breathing the energy toward the crown. Then exhale, while pushing the exhaled air toward your hip. Can you feel your energy traveling through a tunnel from the head to the hips?

- Take three more breaths and feel your inner quiet as you sit.
- Now notice how you feel; do you feel lighter?
- Does your energy feel like it is balanced?

Do this, or any of the other meditations, whenever you feel you need an energy adjustment. All meditations are healing. Pick one that resonates with you. If you cannot meditate for 15-20 minutes, even a two-minute meditation can be incredibly helpful and powerful!

The desired result of every meditation is to align your chakras and aura, to bring them back into balance once more.

Note:

_____

_____

_____

_____

_____

_____

_____

_____

_____

_____

_____

_____

_____

_____

Be in Peace.

Lesson 8:

Be Your Chakras' Best Friend

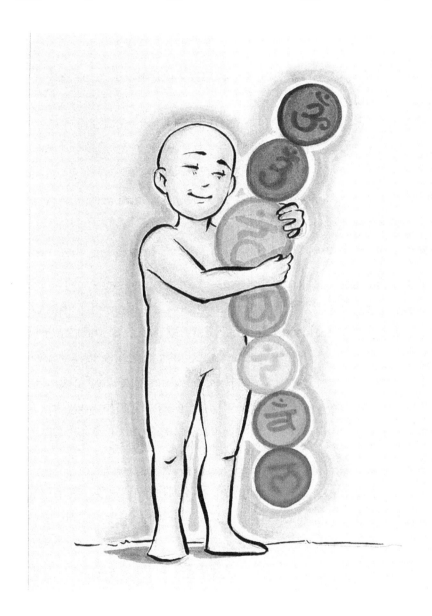

This lesson has many levels of energy medicine concepts that will help you to further understand who you are. To help you to absorb as much of the material as possible, let us start with a grounding and cleansing meditation.

Listen to the meditation here: http://bit.ly/2CkqRiy

Password: Trust

- Find a quiet spot where you will be undisturbed.
- Shut off all electronics.
- Take three cleansing breaths and let go of what you don't need.
- Set a learning intention.
- Quiet your mind every time you have a thought.
- Ask your spirit guides or spirit animal to assist and accompany you in this lesson.
- Play music, if desired.

Best friends are people that you trust with your deepest secrets. They are dependable and reliable; they can be called upon at a moment's notice if you need assistance. They also celebrate your life victories and cheer you on every step of your journey. We all need best friends. By choosing yourself as your very best friend, you're empowered with self-happiness, self-confidence, self-love, a sense of self, and purpose in the world. You are not depended on others for your happiness, approval or validation.

If you are not your own best friend, then who are you? Are you living on the sidelines of your life? I pray NOT! Be honest with yourself. Do you value yourself and believe you deserve love and support? What if you aren't getting emotional support from anywhere else? If you depend on others for your happiness, this sets you up for disappointing expectations.

You may be afraid of failure and embarrassment, but don't let these emotions stop you from making the necessary life changes. Sometimes fear can be so overwhelming that you might find yourself standing on the sidelines of life while waiting for something good to happen to you. Please don't do that. Living on the sideline of life is lonely and depressing.

You deserve everything you desire in life!

Think about how much energy and time you devote to others while sacrificing your own time and energy. By being your own best friend, you can focus on your personal needs and build a foundation of self-esteem before helping others.

Living in your fears and fueling your limited beliefs inhibits your chakras' energy from flowing while slowly extinguishing your inner light. Your chakras will fluctuate between being deficient and excessive energy depending on what your mind convinces you to believe. You aren't doing anyone any favors by keeping your inner light dim.

You can be your own best friend and support your chakras through love, mindfulness, and understanding. Acknowledge your chakras when they feel icky so that they WILL sustain your overall level of energy for everyday living.

Once your chakras are healthy, they will alway have your back! The beauty of having healthy chakras that once you know what they feel like, you will quickly recognize when you are feeling off and you can DO SOMETHING about it before the dark energy sends you spiraling down into a hole.

You CAN and WILL live in a positive and respectful manner.
Be the person you are meant to be!

Our Needs

We, especially women, take care of everyone's needs before we take care of our own. If you are a caregiver, rescuer, homemaker, teacher, or nurturer, people flock to you because you are dependable, and a problem solver. You love taking care of others!

Your natural tendency to offer care is an essential ingredient to feeding your soul. On an unconscious level, you may believe you can care for them better than they care for themselves. Caregivers have a fear of being seen as selfish, but you have every right to practice self-preservation by being a healthy narcissist that can balance giving with receiving.

Learning and knowing what boundaries are, is difficult for the rescuer. Rescuing has become an essential task for those who are addicted to helping others. It can be gratifying, but at the same time, tiring and draining. Most rescuers do not know how to reserve energy for themselves. Instead, they deplete their energy source quicker than it can be replenished. Other than rescuing, what else drains your energy?

PhysicalClutter—
What Does it Do to Your Energy?

To create a healthy and energetic home or work environment, we must be diligent to keep our environment free from clutter. We all have physical clutter, but when it accumulates and piles up in our environment, it also affects the health of our chakras and aura.

Clutter can affect our psyche--it feels very unsettling when things are stacked in piles, and there isn't enough place to put everything. Clutter inhibits Feng Shui energy from moving freely and replaces any open space with stagnant energy. Clutter can make you mad too. One of my pet peeves, I can't stand when good intentional family members bring me bags of groceries. Sounds strange? I don't have space for extra food and get overwhelmed trying to figure out where to put everything. I will even donate extra food because I don't want it to clutter my kitchen, nor do I want the food to go to waste. (Now you know one of my pet peeves.)

Do you feel your stuff owes you? Notice how many things you have that are similar or duplicates. Now is the time to ask yourself why are you filling your life with stuff or junk? Another one of my favorite de-cluttering activities is to donate unused appliances and clothes as soon as they outlive their usefulness.

Clutter is an energy robber, and it can make you feel drained until it is sorted or disposed of. It can steal your inner peace while draining you and making you feel frustrated. This is true especially when you don't know how to organize to get rid of things or where to begin.

Are you holding onto things because you think you will need them again? This may be time to take an inventory of what is stored in the attic and basement? How about clothes that you haven't worn for decades? Are you hoping they come back into fashion? Or are you waiting to fit into them again? Are your possessions taking up too much space and your home is becoming a storage facility?

Confession Time: It took me until my late 40s to donate clothes that I wore in my teens into my 20's. I confess, I still have a pair of size two, very short, pink shorts in my closet that I wore during that time of my life. Even to this day when I look at those shorts, it triggers many fond memories of my youth and being on my honeymoon. On the other hand, I soon donated my wedding dress after my wedding without much thought due to lack of attachment.

Biggest Clutter Drainers

Kitchen cabinets, drawers, and counters — are filled with too many appliances, gadgets, and junk.

Garage/attic— cemetery of forgotten things.

Closet – the average person wears 20% of what is in their closet. Why not donate what you haven't worn for the last two to three years?

Electronics– How many upgrades have you done in the last five years? Do you have a drawer full of dead electronics?

Toys– As a kid, I was happy to get one new toy on my birthday and one at Christmas. Today's kids are barraged with the latest toys and electronics. One of my son's birthday is in December, and I remembered one year he received 40 presents that month. I believe that no child should have that many gifts at one time. Have you tried to convince a seven-year-old child to donate half of his gifts? It doesn't work out too well.

Ask yourself is it time to dispose of clutter that is taking up valuable space? Make time to go through things; sort out what you can let go of. Bless those items and thank them for giving you joy while they were with you. Then send them off to their next destination.

EmotionalClutter–What Does It Do to Us?

After physical clutter takes up physical space, then it begins to take up space in our heads with emotional clutter. We find ourselves spending too much time thinking, analyzing and justifying our purchasing and hoarding habits. Our emotional clutter silently begins to integrate into our belief system by tricking us to believe we need things to help us to feel better about ourselves, but it has the opposite effect instead. Emotional clutter steals our peace and leaves a void because we don't feel good about ourselves and we replace our feelings useless things and thoughts.

We do many things to distract us from our void. We waste our time by doing too much or making half-hearted commitments. Or we numb ourselves with destructive activities such as recreational drugs, alcohol, overeating, etc. Or we indulge in other activities to avoid looking at ourselves, until one day these empty activities no longer work and then you are forced to look at yourself.

Many of us are not aware of the garbage we have held onto since childhood, nor would we know what to do with it if we realized it. When the pain becomes too much, then it is time to transform these emotions with love and compassion.

Emotional Clutter Busters

Evaluating emotional clutter is the same as assessing physical clutter. Make a list of emotions that haven't serve you in a long time. Ask yourself why are you holding on to them or why are you repeating the same lesson? Now commit to learning how to let them go.

Steps to releasing physical and emotional clutter (please be honest):

What are you stuffing your life with?

_____

_____

What are you hiding from?

_____

_____

What are you avoiding?

_____

_____

_____

What emotions are you ready to let go?

_____

_____

_____

When Something Doesn't Feel Right

Here are three levels of emotional blockages (feel free to add your own:

- What is it that doesn't feel right?
- Who, what, and why does it disturb me?
- What do I need to do to fix the problem?

Emotions are trapped energy within the physical body. These feelings prevent us from connecting with others on an emotional level. It can also cause us to become emotionally numb as a means of coping with anxiety and nervousness. Long-term unresolved emotional blockages can and usually, manifest into physical and mental problems.

If you notice, triggers are usually about the same unresolved conflicts. In the meantime, we spin our wheels or bang our heads trying to figure it out why we still have a problem. Most of us don't like confrontations. It is hard to use our voices in a way that do not sound defensive and judgmental.

Our words become stuck in our throats. What makes the problem worse, the person is who is triggering our emotions isn't aware that we have a problem since there has been no indication of a problem.

Understanding your emotions and where they are coming from is an empowering step for change.

Honesty

If you need help to recognize and talk about your voids; work with a professional to help you discover what you are avoiding. If you aren't interested in talking to a licensed therapist, try journaling. I have always found writing to be helpful. Your soul will tell you the truth, if only you will listen.

It's time to let go of stored physical junk and emotional junk. Move forward to make room for the things that are working for you. If you are moving ahead too fast, you can always slow it down, but you can't move forward by standing still. I doubt that you will want to interrupt momentum once you taste what true emotional and energetic freedom feels like.

Take responsibility for your health, life path and joy!

How Do We Dialogue with Others?

There are many ways that we talk with each other. The way we engage in conversation can either support or disrupt our energy flow. Unfortunately, many of us say things without awareness, lack of respect, or integrity. Then we wonder why we get the responses that we do and become hurt by words and reactions.

There are four levels of conversation. The deeper the level of conversation, the more conscious and open we are. Some of these levels are:

Informational — When we first meet someone we usually engage in general non-threatening, small talk, such as "How is the weather? What is your favorite season?" This type of conversation gives you a chance to get to know someone by feeling their essence and gathering information about them through their voice, tone, body language, eye contact, etc.

Personal or Emotional — You begin to share more personal information during conversations, such as "How do you *feel* about the weather? What is your favorite sport and why do you enjoy it?" This type of communication helps you to practice your active listening skills while getting to know the person on a different level.

Relational — You begin to focus on how you and the other person feel and behave. The relationship becomes more profound, and you are more aware of the other person's feelings and may ask personal questions such as, "I noticed that something is bothering you, do you want to talk about it?"

Non-Verbal — Communication doesn't have to be done through words; a look, a gesture, or a movement can be just powerful as words.

Energy Draining Dialogues

Venting — Venting is a brief release to get something off one's chest, or to blow off steam. It can be a healthy way to express suppressed emotions. If you are a person, who likes to vent, be careful when and how often you vent. Many are not aware of the effect venting has on the receiver that is being "energetically dumped on" or "energetically thrown up on." Alternatively, this is usually a one-sided dialogue exchange, where the venting person talks so much that the other person can't squeeze in a word edgewise. The person venting has entered the "Energy Vampire Zone."

EnergyVampires-WhoAreThey?

Energy vampires can be anyone--your family, friends, co-workers, colleagues, and even strangers. These people are emotionally immature who believe the world revolves around their views. After an encounter with one, you may feel drained, stupid, unworthy, offended, defensive, challenged, or physically sick. Energy vampires cannot create or sustain their life energy in a positive manner, so they latch onto and feed off of other people's energy as they are slowly suck the life out of others.

Energy Vampire example — I had dinner with an acquaintance whom I hadn't seen in a while. She took a phone call, and after she hung up, she proceeded to vent about the person on the phone and what she did wrong. After listening for 10 minutes, I asked her, "Why did you assume I wanted to hear about that person's story?" My friend was taken aback by my question. We both thought the other was rude.

What I hoped to achieve was to make her aware why she felt compelled to tell me about a stranger's mishaps. A stranger that I most likely will never meet. She continued to go on and state how she would have handled the situation differently, regardless if I wanted to hear it or not. What she was doing was talk for the sake of talking, without value or direction. (See the Ramble description below.) As I listened, I felt my energy dwindling.

Since I had nothing to add to the story, I decided that I didn't want to hear the story anymore; it served no purpose for me to know. I asked her to stop telling her story. That moment became very quiet and awkward for the both of us. My lesson here is: I utilized my throat chakra to protect my aura and my chakras. What I hope she learned is not to feel the urge to talk, or gossip, about a stranger's circumstance for no reason other than to vent her frustrations.

Complainer — The complainer is passive, has stagnant energy, and wallows in pity. The act of complaining becomes hardwired in the brain in a permanent dissatisfaction pattern. It takes less energy to be harmful than to be positive. Many of us have no idea that complaining has a significant impact on our mental and physical health. While complaining, your body overworks by releasing stress hormones from your adrenals to calm you down.

The next time you start to complain, stop your negative thoughts from taking over and ask yourself:

- Why am I complaining?
- What am I dissatisfied with?
- How often do I complain? If you don't know, ask your friends for an honest assessment of how often you complain.
- Do I also complain to strangers? I see this all the time while waiting to check out at the supermarket. If you complain this way, you have crossed boundaries, and you are an Energy Vampire.
- How can I turn my complaints into solutions?
- How can I change my attitude!

Rambler — The Rambler will repeat the same story while conveying no useful information. They take up your time and your mental space. They are usually NOT interested in having a dialogue exchange. These people repeat the same old stories because they don't have new stories to share. Somewhere in their life, they became energetically stuck. This can happen for many reasons, such as aging, health issues, traumatic experiences, moving to a new home, losing friends, retirement, the death of a spouse, or ignoring emotions or just wired differently. Often these people can voice their frustrations while venting and complaining within the same conversation.

Always protect your aura!

196

Inactive Listener — Most of us don't listen. We hear what we want to hear and then zone out the rest. Active listening is more than just hearing words; it is processing what we hear while feeling the other person's emotions, and seeing their views. When actively listening, we have a dialogue exchange in which each person is sincerely interested in what the other has to say.

Stop the Negative Talk Action Plan

A powerful action plan begins with a clear purpose, vision, or goal. Action plans are designed to take you from where you are now to where you want to be. You can achieve any goal you set out to accomplish with time and commitment. You will have mostly good days, and you will have days when you are off. Accept yourself for where you are and don't judge yourself when things aren't going well. Continue with your journey regardless of how you feel. Don't allow negative feelings to take root in your chakras.

Jot down your thoughts or create a vision board. Get a planner (there are plenty on the internet and in stores) to set and remind you of your goals.

List your thoughts, ideas and what you want to accomplish. It is easy to give lip service to your vision, but once on paper, it is another story. It becomes a commitment. The clearer you are with your vision and what are the steps to get there, the higher the chance of success.

Identify your task. Can you see the big picture but don't know how to get there? Break tasks down into small, doable steps.

Set daily/weekly/monthly schedules.. Be realistic about your tasks and what you can do. Schedule your tasks. On my daily to-do list, I write six things that I would like to achieve, but I am satisfied with completing the top three. Prioritizing is a must. I have to let go of the other three and work on them another time (don't forget to put it on your calendar.) Permit yourself NOT to feel bad when you fall behind.

Schedule specification. Put a date on it. All the hoping and wishing in the world won't get you there. Sorry.

Block off personal time. Stop sabotaging yourself by doing too much and over-committing. Exhaustion and confusion only set you up to fail. We all want to be "super" people, but devoting time to family and friends and reserving quiet time for yourself is equally critical as completing tasks.

Let patience be your teacher. Don't get discouraged if you do not see progress as quickly as you like. It takes time and patience to build a sustainable foundation of energy. I have been working on my energy goals since 1992, and I am *still* building my foundation. I have accepted the pace I am going, and even if I want to go faster, the door to opportunity will NOT open any sooner until I have mastered the task at hand. Patience has taught me resilience to build a stronger inner core.

Highlight milestones. Check everything off as you go and give yourself a high-five every time you accomplish a task. Please acknowledge every successful step. Too often we gloss over our achievements while we check off our list.

I Don't Want to Do It Anymore!

What is your program? What changes can you sincerely make and with a whole heart? We make promises to ourselves, but we negate on our promises. Often, the excuse will be, "I will do _____ when the kids leave home or when I retire." I have never been able to define what is a perfect time. I can sense when it is a better time, but there is NO such thing as an ideal time.

Validate Yourself— Are you waiting for someone to give you permission to live your life? Has waiting made you feel angry, bitter and resentful? Everyone wants to be seen, heard, and validated, but don't rely on others tell you how, and when to live. Listen to what they have to say, but then decide what is right for you. Most of the time, they are unconsciously telling you why they are fearful of making changes in their own lives.

We all HAVE inner wisdom! It is a matter of recognizing, listening, and then follow through with an action plan. Stop thinking that you are letting yourself down. Everything is about perspective. Too often we wish for things that are just a fingertip away, but we are afraid to extend our hand. Life can be like a TV show, if you don't like what you see, then change the channel.

> *"You have been criticizing yourself for years, and it hasn't worked. Try approving of yourself and see what happens."*
> —*Louise Hay*

Expectations — Our expectations are so ingrained that we become easily disappointed and hurt when something doesn't turn out the way we planned. Expectations are happiness killers. They keep us from living in the moment and being joyful because the need to control outcomes are more important than being happy. If your world is full of inflexibility, an unexpected curve ball can send you down into a rabbit hole of darkness. I am still learning how to let go of expectations; something I have been working on for my life. You may be wondering doesn't everyone have expectations. The answer is "yes," but the key is whether you can be flexible if something doesn't work out as planned.

No one can hurt you the way you can hurt yourself! Believe that you ARE the best that you are. When we learn to accept ourselves and our situations, we can be grateful for what we have. Let go of unrealized expectations and enjoy your life instead of waiting for something that may never come.

Stop Waiting and Start Living!

I Don't Feel Alive Anymore?

Don't let your emotions turn into anger, bitterness, and resentment. These feelings can turn into rage. If you are reliving the same story repeatedly in your mind, stop and ask yourself how your tale is fueling your emotions. Are your stories real? Do you blame others for your misfortunes? Any story we tell ourselves enough time, we can make it be our truth.

These types of lash-outs lower our self-esteem and we believe we don't deserve any better. This trapped dark energy acts the same way as Post Traumatic Stress Disorder (PTSD) and becomes embedded deeply into our cellular level until we accept these emotions as normalcy. To protect ourselves from feeling these painful emotions we numb out these emotions or erase them from our minds.

Get help! You don't have to suffer in silence. If you have old wounds that haven't been addressed, you can do something about this. There are many professional people who can help you to identify and heal your physical and emotional pain so that you can heal.

Quiet Down the Ego — When I am feeling blue, reflections and meditation help to quiet the negative chatter in my head. My focus is to mute my ego while I check to see why I am out of the flow.

The ego is the false sense of self. It wants to tell you why you are imperfect, why you will never succeed, and why you are wrong in 10,000 ways. You can learn to override negative thoughts by NOT believing your thoughts. You are the one who let these thoughts take root. Your soul wants to mentor and guide you towards healing. It is a matter of learning to listen to yourself and then following through with your suggestions. My quiet time is critical to me; it connects me to my spirit, to the divine, and to my inner wisdom.

How to Break Negative Energy Patterns

By connecting with your soul, together, you will break your negative energy patterns while helping you through difficult times. For some, this is a time to connect with God or the universe. By becoming friends with your negativity, you can use it as a tool for growth. If you listen to your negativity, it will teach you what life lessons you still need to learn. It can even tell you your purpose in life. When we ignore these messages, it alienates us from everything, including ourselves.

Be Proactive! Support Your Emotional Energy

Get enough rest. It is a blessing to be able to get a good night of sleep. During a restful night of sleep, your body is replenishing its energy source and healing itself. Even if we want to stay up and party, you are doing your body a disservice by working against your internal clock.

Get enough movement time. There are days I want to sit in front of the TV and vegged out. I know I can't. My body requires a lot of movement. For me, lack of movement transfers into sluggish and dense energy. One of the reasons why I have puppies that they force me to get out of my chair and take them out for walks. Have you noticed how you feel when you haven't moved enough? Does your energy feel heavy? What happens when you miss several days of working out? If I don't move, I can feel the results within 48 hours. Your body is meant for moving.

Eat a healthy diet. I'm at the age I feel resentful that I can't eat what I want, and whenever I want. I should be able to! There are days I dream of fried clams and rice noodle dishes. Unfortunately, my waistline and my energy don't allow these temptations often. I know when I have eaten the wrong foods; my stomach (3rd chakra) and intestines (2nd chakra) feels stuffy and bloated. My energy then moves like sludge.

Do regular check-ins. Know your energy flow to prevent energy crashes. Don't wait for a melt down to happen before checking in.

Activities - As mentioned, my favorite "me" time is walking with my puppies and being in nature. I love trees and flowers. Many times I will sit with my back up against a tree and ask the trees to take away my physical and emotional pain. (Something I have done since my hippie days.) Trees are pure energy, and they can transform pain into pure energy. This act does not hurt the trees.

Accept life events as lessons, instead of viewing them as punishments. Your resistance to learning may be the cause of continuously repeating the same painful life experiences. By chance, did you see the movie "Groundhog Day?" Did you notice how frustrated and disenchanted the main character, Phil Connors, played by Bill Murray was? An arrogant Pittsburgh TV Weatherman was covering the annual Groundhog Day event in Punxsutawney, Pennsylvania. Phil found himself caught in a time loop containing his miserable life, job, his disdain for people and his world. Every day repeated precisely as it did before until he learned the lesson and to see the needs of others before his own needs. By breaking his pity cycle, the day rebooted and started afresh.

If you are a member of your own pity party, it is time to leave it and take another path. You are the ONLY person that can make changes in your life. NO white knight is coming to save you.

Establish your boundaries. Know what you will and will NOT do. Choose not to live a Ground Hog Day life.

Homework—Be Your Best Friend

Everyone has days when they don't feel like getting out of bed. Everything feels off, and don't know why. Sometimes we lose connections to ourselves, family, friends, and to the divine. Often, these feelings come from the closed or weakened aura and chakras. By keeping your energy balanced and healthy, your chakras and aura appreciate your support so that they can continue to generate the energetic output to meet your challenges.

Chakras and auras are subtle energies, influenced by mental, emotional, physical, and spiritual information. By understanding and respecting your chakras and aura, you will quickly know when something is out of balance, and you can do something about it instead of waiting to see what happens next.

It is not unusual for chakras to become unbalanced hundreds of times a day, especially if your aura is fragile. All it takes is a disagreement or a conflict; then suddenly these emotional attacks weaken the aura and cause the chakras to become chaotic while looking for direction from you to correct the energy flow. It is simple to replenish the chakra energy once you know how. It is just a matter of training and conditioning chakras the same way you would train for a 5K race.

Breaking negative cycles takes time, but once broken, **you are no longer a prisoner of your emotions.** Keep working on it. Just think of how far you have come in a few lessons. In time, you will be able to change your current emotional default program to a new program that always supports you.

Questions to Think About --

These questions will encourage you to let go of the past and give yourself permission to break the punishment cycle:

Of all the energy personality traits listed, which traits do you identify with?

_____

Which ones triggered your emotions?

_____

How do you normally respond in a difficult situation?

_____

What do you do to defuse the pain?

_____

Which chakra feels the pain the most?

_____

How do you care for your hurt chakra?

_____

What self care practice do you implement the most?

_____

Do you recognize when you have emotional releases?

_____

Notes:

_____

_____

_____

Heal Your Soul Meditation

This meditation will release any negative emotions on a cellular level so that deep healing will begin. You will meet with each chakra, then acknowledge it, and tell it what a super job it is doing.

Listen to the meditation here: http://bit.ly/2B04jmV

Password: Super

The rules are the same as the grounding and cleansing meditation at the beginning of the lesson.

Place open hands, face up on your lap. Plant your feet on the floor with your shoes on or off.

Take three cleansing breaths, breath in through your nose and exhale out through your mouth.

First or Root Chakra

Check in and just feel your first chakra. Your first chakra represents your security around your home, family, work, food, love, joy, health, and abundance. See if the energy is balanced. If not, turn the energy control knob to the right for more energy or to the left for less.

Give your first chakra a high five. Say: *Thank you for giving me so much by helping me stay balanced.* Be grateful for everything that is going on in your life, no matter how small. Voice at least one thing you are grateful for. Be appreciative for all that your chakras do for you.

Take three cleansing breaths.

Second or Emotion Chakra

Place both hands palm down underneath the belly button. Take a deep breath through your nose and exhale through your mouth until you feel the exhaled breath pushing against your hands.

Now check in with the energy to see if it is balanced. If not, turn the energy knob to the right for more energy or to the left for less.

Give your second chakra some appreciation. Thank it for helping you to feel and process emotions on WHATEVER level you are comfortable with.

Acknowledge it for all your achievements. Feel the energy. Feel how juicy it is. Thank it for the life you have, your loves, and all the people and things you are connected to. Focus on how you feel about them and yourself.

Take three cleansing breaths.

Third or Self Esteem Chakra

 Bring your hands to your third chakra right underneath your rib cage. Take a deep breath through your nose and exhale through your mouth until you feel the exhaled breath pushing against your hands.

Now check in with the energy to see if it is balanced. If not, turn the energy knob to the right for more energy or to the left for less.

Acknowledge your self-esteem. Feel how good it is to be in your body. Appreciate your condition. However, you may feel. Don't judge it to be one way or another. Love your power. Love who you are. Love everything you do including your mistakes. Thank your third chakra.

Take three cleansing breaths.

Fourth or Heart Chakra

 Place your hands on your heart or envision placing your hands on your heart while you rest your hands in your lap.

You have a big heart. Sometimes it feels a little beaten because you don't love yourself enough, or you have take yourself for granted. Appreciate the love that you have for all, including yourself. There is no one like you. Think of all the beautiful things you do for others.

Good job.

Check in with the energy to see if your heart is balanced. If not, turn the energy knob to the right for more energy or to the left for less.

Take three cleansing breaths.

Fifth or Throat Chakra

Place your hands on your throat heart or envision placing your hands on your throat while you rest your hands in your lap.

Many people have problems with this chakra, but it doesn't mean that this chakra is more important than the others. This chakra can hold years of stifled and painful words. You're going to let those words out. Let them be free by voicing them out loud. If you need to, shout them out. You don't have to say things in a negative tone. There are ways to deliver thoughtful words. Find what's right for you. If your words are for someone else, think about how you would say them. Many times, the other person is just nervous and anxious as you are. He or she doesn't know what to say either. Confrontations are never easy. Words can be delivered in loving, constructive, and supportive manner.

Check in with the energy to see if your throat chakra is balanced. If not, turn the energy knob to the right for more energy or to the left for less.

You have it in you and now to let them out. Don't let negative energy be your default communication mode. Find a different way. Change your attitude, and the frequency and tone of the words will change too. You will know when you are using the right words. You will feel it.

Take three cleansing breaths.

Sixth or Third Eye Chakra

Place your hands on your third eye or envision placing your hands on your third eye while your hands are resting in your lap. Take a deep breath through your nose and exhale through your mouth until you feel the exhaled breath pushing against your hands.

Now check in with the energy to see if it is balanced. If not, turn the energy knob to the right for more energy or to the left for less.

Your intuition is continually sharing subtle information with you about what is going on in your life. It wants to support you so that you will make thoughtful decisions, to be JOYFUL, and not just to GET THROUGH the day.

Your intuition is always guiding you. Learn to listen to that quiet inner voice, and dare yourself to follow through. You are wiser than you know. You have all of the universe's knowledge within you.

All the small things you're obsessing over, come from unfounded fears and non-supported perceptions. See yourself in your light. Don't let other people's judgment affect you. They, too, are afraid. Not only are you helping yourself but you are also helping the other person.

Take three cleansing breaths.

Seventh or Crown Chakra

 Place your hands on the top of your head, or envision placing your hands on your crown while your hands are resting in your lap. Take a deep breath through your nose and exhale through your mouth until you feel the exhaled breath pushing against your hands.

Now check in with the energy to see if it is balanced. If not, turn the energy knob to the right for more energy or to the left for less.

Be open to receiving messages from your higher self, or from God, the universe, spirit animals, or spirit guides; they are all on your team. They all want to serve you, guide you, and to give you wisdom. Make use of their support. Don't entertain doubts. Instead, feel your power.

Take three cleansing breaths.

On your last exhale, envision exhaling air from your crown while pushing it toward your first chakra. Take another breath in and, as you exhale, envision pushing negative energy out of your aura in a three-hundred-and-sixty-degree fashion (from all external body surfaces.)

How do you feel? Better? Quieter? Lighter? Please reread this lesson several times until you feel that the energy of the words penetrates into your cellular body and you can feel negativity dissolving.

Now that you know the many ways of how to be your chakras' best friend. You have sustainable and skills to protect them. You are your chakras' best friend.

Be the queen or king of your universe.
Trust your inner self and the divine to guide you.

Lesson 9:

Protect Your Precious Energy Resources

Your energy resources increase and decrease depending on how mindfully you manage your energy. Mindfulness is being aware of your body and noticing when something doesn't feel right and then work to bring your body back to balance. When your energetic system is operating optimally, it will sound an alert when negativity has infiltrated your chakras.

It takes discipline to be mindful. Humans are habitual creatures. We value our routines regardless if they good or bad practices for us. Many think mindfulness is a new age practice, but being mindful means that we are consciously aware of what is going on in our lives. Once it is decided to live a conscious life, it will take time before the practice becomes habitual.

Our ability to manage our energy will continuously be tested. Think of who and what triggers our emotions and fears. For example, I met a man who wanted to sell me a marketing program for a hefty price. The plan sounded fantastic, but it was more than I could afford. The man went on and on telling me why I needed this program, and I almost said yes, but my chakras were telling me not to do it. I could have easily ignored my chakras, but I decided to trust my gut and said, "No, thank you." All I heard from the man was, "but, but, but..." I have no regrets about saying no. In fact, I don't remember the man's name, his company or what the marketing program he was selling. I knew I made the right decision. Listening and following through with what I feel is vital to supporting my chakras.

We all have self-doubt. No one is exempt from it, but we CAN control how fearful we become. It is amazing how fear can overtake us. Self-doubt starts as off as a whisper, then gets louder, telling us why we are not good enough or why we will never get ahead. This inner dialogue turns our heads into a war zone, where doubt is the only winner. We have the power to stop this destructive dialogue before it escalates.

Take 5

Think about your doubts--What have they taught you? Have they attracted negative outcomes or taught you valuable life skill lessons? Yes, doubts can be positive or negative depending on how you view them.

- Which fears keep coming up?
- What have you done to tame them?
- What do you want? Put it out in the universe and ask for what you want!

Yes, ask what you want and be bold about it!

What do you want? Set the intention of attracting and receiving it. Don't be obsessive or continually express your desires. The law of attraction works better if you can voice your wishes once, and then move on. Let your words do their magic. Imagine, like a feather blowing and floating with the wind, your words have the same powerful energy and movement while waiting for the right time to sprout and grow your desires.

Our insecurities and self-doubt keep us from getting what we want. Too many times we want change to happen, but we become afraid, or anxious about how much time and money it is going to take to make it happen. Because of our fears, we end up sabotaging ourselves by not taking the next step. It is always easier to live with our discomforts than go outside of our comfort zone. Everything begins with the first step. No amount of wishing or hoping will grant a desire if there is a conflict when your thoughts and actions are not in alignment with each other.

It is time to stop giving away your powers and listen to your inner voice. Trust yourself! Don't hide behind your darkness and don't use it as an excuse for not living.

Grounding and Cleansing Meditation

Listen to the meditation here: http://bit.ly/2B1ji0g

Password: Energy

General Meditation Rules

- Find a quiet and undisturbed spot.
- Shut off all electronics.
- Take three cleansing breaths and let go of what you don't need.
- Set your intention what you want to get out of the lesson.
- Quiet down your mind's chatter.
- Ask your spirit guides or spirit animal to assist and accompany you during the lesson.
- Play music, if desired.

How have your circumstances affected your world? There are many thought-provoking questions in this lesson that will teach how you navigated through your everyday situations.

How Do You See Your World?

Your world is a somewhat new concept, but it is also an ageless question. While some have easily and successfully obtain all of life comforts, then there are others who struggle to have enough.

Walt Disney — "If you can dream it, you can do it."

Oprah Winfrey — "Remember, you are co-creating your life with the energy of your own intentions."

You are the only one who can shape your reality. Somewhere within you, find the power to sculpture your life. Many believe we have a few life choices or no control over our lives. We go along and accept ordinary living, but this isn't true. We all have life options, but few want to exercise their options because it is too much work or there is too much fear of the unknown. We all have emotional baggage that stops us from moving ahead. You can override the blame, forgive your life circumstances, and choose how much emotional baggage you want to carry. Time alone doesn't always heal all; it is your choice how to heal your wounds.

Take more than 5

Here are questions to help you determine how your inner energy default program was installed. Answer them as honestly can you can.

- Are you more positive than negative?
- Do you see the best in situations or the worse?
- Do you feel safe?
- Do you feel supported and loved?
- Do you love yourself enough to make yourself number one?
- Are you easily influenced by what people say about you?
- Whom do you blame for your problems?
- Have you learned anything from your problems?
- If you could choose a different outcome, what would that be?

I know these are hard questions. Please put your thoughtful responses in your journal. If you don't know who you are, then no one else will know either. Once you know your truth, you can then live an authentic and transparent life instead of a life filled with self-doubt and fear.

What Messages/Vibes Does Your Aura Broadcast?

Do you know what information your aura is transmitting? Is it a positive or negative vibration? We broadcast messages 24-7, consciously and unconsciously. Your aura is a multipurpose broadcasting system that receives, collects, and processes information from every experience you had.

When your aura becomes overloaded with too much information, this is when you begin to feel tired, overwhelmed, and confused. Think about how you feel at the end of a workday? Drained? Have you wasted your time? Now is the time to evaluate how you want to invest your energy?

Who is Judging You?

No one is judging or looking at you the way you think they are. Everyone is distracted by their worries that they don't have enough energy to worry about you. Your inner judge, judges you the most.

My elderly mother still worries about being judged even though most of her friends have passed on. Judgment has caused her a lifetime of anxiety. One occasion, I asked her, "What are you so worried about now that most of your friends have passed on" Her response, "I don't know anymore." What this tells me that her fear of being judged is profound and deeply ingrained in her soul level that she still worries about what her living friends think about her. I told her that her friends were worried about their problems and they aren't looking to add her problems to their lists.

We must stop self-defeating behavior.

Stop the Negativity

We all have an inner loop of negative thoughts that run in our heads. The encoding began when we were kids. Most negativity is attached to unrealized expectations. Expectations are things we are supposed to do or are good at, such as being an obedient son or daughter, be a successful student, be a hard worker, be a loving mom/dad, be good providers, and the list goes on. If we can't live up to our expectations, they become stressors and anxiety-inducing emotions.

What keeps us from moving ahead in our lives are our fears of:

Making a mistake — Everyone is afraid of making mistakes and being reprimanded. When you were a child, how often did your parents, elders, and teachers correct you when you made mistakes? Did they do it kindly or did they embarrassed or shamed you? How did it make you feel? Did you think you couldn't do anything right? You might think because you made so many mistakes that you are stupid and no one loves you. You will never get ahead in life. Did you learned from your mistakes or have they kept you too fearful to move ahead?

Being Rejected — Everyone wants to be accepted, valued and seen. Rejection is the most common emotional we experience throughout our lives. Not everyone is going to like us, or agree with us or see our views. In the past, we would pick up the phone or meet to talk and communicate our differences. Today, live conversations have been replaced by electronic communication and social media, thus creating more misunderstanding and more opportunities to be rejected.

Not good enough?— We are afraid of never living up to someone's or even to our own expectations; we remember a parent or teacher pushing us too hard and told us that we could have done better. Leaving us feeling that our results are never good enough.

219

Change— If we are insecure, always fearful of failing, or don't have enough courage to move on. We end up living a status quo life instead.

What if You are Good Enough Exactly as You are in this Moment?

Now that we live in a digital age, people are continually announcing their significant life events on various social media platforms, leaving many to feel inadequate. We feel a need to compete or to keep up. It is easy to forget that the lives people present online are curated to show only the ideal parts while the ordinary and challenging moments are conveniently edited out.

The reality is that everyone struggles on some level. By focusing on the positive aspects of your life rather than the false comparisons, you will live a happier, more authentic, and vibrant life instead.

Here is a personal story I would like a share ...

I admit I do a lot in a day. I can easily do the work of two people. I am blessed with a tremendous amount of energy. Along with working hard, I also have many hobbies that I enjoy, such as cooking, baking, knitting, and exercising. In fact, if I didn't have to sleep, I would do more, but I have to listen to my body when it tells me to stop and rest.

People who know me always tell me that I do too much in a day. I sense that they would like to do more, but they respect their limitations. It is not my intent to make what I do a competition. I often hear comments like "I had a productive Helen Day." At first, I didn't know what that meant; in fact, I was insulted. What they were saying to me that they were pleased with the amount of work and tasks completed that day.

What I heard and internalized was, "Why do I drive yourself so hard? Do I think my self-worth is connected to how much I can do or produce? Do I keep myself so busy that I don't have to think about anything else other than what has to be done?" I had no real answers.

I remembered feeling angry when being viewed as a "productivity" model. My response was "Believe me; you don't want to be me! I drive myself so crazy thinking what needs to get done every day and then working obsessively to get my task list checked off.

I also finally realized why I keep so busy— I was in competition with myself to get as much done as much as possible in the shortest amount of time. I was too rigid with my check list and commitments. I finally learned how to cut myself some slack if I couldn't check off everything on my to-do list. I no longer feel guilty about it.

The message behind the story is that we don't know what anyone goes through and what they think. What appears to be peaceful on the outside can be a tortuous internal conflict.

STOP trying to walk in someone else's shoes. It is time to fill your own!

Your perception — Everyone has unique perceptions. No two people will experience or see things in the same way. Your attitudes are defined by the way you interpret information and then deciding what to believe. Forming perceptions is like writing a screenplay; you can make the theme happy and lighthearted, or dark and depressing. You are the director of your impressions. Yes, you can choose your theme and whatever subject you want your life to be, and then live it!

Self-sabotage — Now imagine that your movie is playing. You like your life, but there are some days you don't see the positives, so you make up something that is dark and ugly to eat away at your joy. It takes work to have a happy life; many things are overwhelming. It takes more energy to succeed than it does to fail. You become tired and flustered; then the self-saboteur tells you that no one can be positive all the time and that you don't have enough energy to keep going.

Suddenly, the cycle of negativity begins, and your inner dialogue turns down a dark path, telling you that "*you are right and you can't go on like this!*" Before you know, your perception begins telling you that nothing you do is real and everything is a charade. Instead of letting your dark side take over, recognize your dark ego is doing the talking. You can override the dark conversation in your head.

Everyone has a self-saboteur; the goal is not to allow it slip in and dictate your life when your energy is flagging. Be aware when the darkness begins to creep in and do something about it before it takes hold of you. We all have dark days, but only you can keep your darkness in its place.

Introducing Your Authentic Self to the World

As your chakras become healthier and stronger, many changes will occur. Most changes will be positive, and some unexpectedly not so. Most likely you will feel uplifted, and your energy frequency will attract new opportunities, outcomes, and friends, while you find that your impressions, views, and attitudes will change, too.

These changes may threaten or disconcert family members and friends because the role you play in their lives is changing. They feel displaced and uncertain of what is going on. Suddenly, these people don't fit into your life the way they used to, and it is stressful for everyone as they are figuring out what their new roles are. You will notice as your energy frequency changes, most likely the other people's frequency will remain the same (unless they choose to grow with you.) You will begin to see and treat people differently because your views will also change. You may want to maintain the relationships, or you find you have outgrown each other. Outgrowing someone is a painful component of personal growth work, but it happens often. If these people are valuable to you and you want to keep them in your life, there some things you can do to support the relationship. Such as -

- Talk about your feelings and the recent changes in your relationship. Take time to hear their feelings as well as sharing your own.
- Keep them in your life, but in a different role. Reinventing relationships are complicated, especially if you are the one that has changed.
- Invite them to join you on your journey. Not everyone is ready to do personal process work, and this is also a big responsibility.
- Move on. It might be time to part ways. It is always sad when a relationship expires, but sometimes it is the healthiest way forward.

On a personal note - At the beginning of my journey in 2004, I had a good friend whose company I enjoyed very much. We are both avid and passionate knitters. For eighteen years, we would travel several times a year to various knitting venues. Then I began to notice in the last two years of our relationship it started to change and we were growing a part. It wasn't anything either one of us did or said, but our encounters became distant and cold until it severed utterly. Even though I reached out to her several times, she decided not to continue with our friendship. I knew at the time I was shifting and growing, and our energy was no longer compatible. We were vibrating at a different frequency. Our relationship felt different and strained. Instead of feeling bitter about parting ways, I am grateful for the years we shared together.

Overcome Negativity

It's time to take back your power. It is your right to be who you are without worrying about what other people think of you. *We give away our powers too quickly to appease others.* But why? Do we look to others for approval? Do they hold some power over us? Do they know more than we do? Are they more important than we are?

STOP! Don't give power to these questions by answering them! *No one has this kind of power over you*! Many of us that are new to the consciousness game and we don't know what is expected of us--the rules change all of the time. Who makes up the rules? We do! How have your rules served you? Instead of being a rule keeper, be a ruler changer! Look at how your rules have kept you from moving forward. Now is the time to make a change.

Instead of processing your feelings with your brain, can you do it from your heart? Work with your chakras instead of fighting with them. You already have the inner wisdom and knowledge but you have forgotten how to use those skills. Trust and believe in yourself!

Begin to appreciate the beauty of your life. You are an exquisite human being. There is no one else like you. No one, yourself included, can make you feel stupid unless you allow it to happen.

Below is a mantra to help change your energetic frequency to attract what you want in your life. When we first start to recite mantras, we voice them in doubt. When repeated hundreds of times, your energetic being will believe what is being said. **Activity** - To deepen the energy of mantras, stand in front of a mirror and repeat mantras while looking at yourself in the mirror until you can feel the energy penetrating your soul. This exercise is hard to do for most. It will take a while before you believe what you are saying. (More thoughts on mantras below.)

Love Myself Mantra

I love myself.
I am unique. There is no one like me.
I believe in myself.
I am mighty.
I have unlimited energy.
I am resourceful.
I am blessed.
I take back my power!

There are many ways to support your body and your energy. Much has to do with your attitude, your desires, and recognizing where you are right now and where you want to go.

Gratitude — Every morning get out of bed and voice what you are grateful for. You can express your gratitude out loud or silently. Next, set the intention for your day. An intention can be as simple as, "I will have a peaceful day or I will be loving or I will have enough time." You will be surprised how intentions can set a high vibrational tone for the entire day and deflect negativity. Be grateful for the smallest of things.

Today I am grateful for

1.

_____

2.

_____

3.

_____

4.

_____

Eat better— For positive energy flow, eat an alkaline diet consisting of fruits and vegetables that are nutrient-dense. Don't overeat. It is best to eat only when you are hungry. Learn your body's signals; it will tell you when you need nourishment. Eliminate processed and fast foods, restrict sugar, dairy, carbohydrates, meat, and alcohol. Remember, junk food produces junk energy.

Be in nature — Go out and see the sun instead of looking at the sun through your window. Enjoy a walk, get some fresh air, and to meditate among trees and flowers, or even snowy woodlands. Get up early to appreciate a sunrise or sit quietly to watch a sunset. Really look and take in your surroundings.

Move your body and drive your energy through your chakras and out of your aura — Do any form of movement that makes you happy and light--tennis, walking, kickboxing, yoga–whatever keeps you moving and motivated. If you can, devote a minimum of one hour or more a day to a routine. That would be great!

Make memories by doing and NOT by wishing — Don't put off doing something with excuses. Do things that will grow your happiness NOW.

Rituals — What are your rituals? After my hard day of work, I love coming home to cook for my family, and then working out. My favorite end of the day reward is taking a long soaking bath with bath salts to help me release and wash away my tensions. (By the way, bath salts help to cleanse the aura. You can use any type of salt. Depending on the size of your tub, use a handful to a cupful.)

Be kind to yourself on those days when you feel off balance — This is how you practice being your chakras' best friend. Appreciate yourself. Take the time to rest and ground yourself as needed. If you are having a quiet day, enjoy the time off and don't look for things to do.

Practice Self-Care:

Manage your stress — Give yourself calm and quiet time in the morning before you go to work and also at the end of the day to eliminate any negativity you might have picked up or are experiencing.

Surround yourself with positive people — Who doesn't want to be surrounded by positive and uplifting people? You know who they are and you know which people suck the life out of you. Be around those who support you and see you for who you are, instead of what you can do for them. Find and build your community.

Make time for yourself — Care for yourself the way you would care for others. I call this "my time." Make time to instill peace in yourself. I love when I can sit quietly without the television on and keep myself company. I'm not doing anything during these times other than just enjoying the quiet and sitting still. It took me five years to learn how to sit quietly (I'm glad it only took me five years!)

Love and respect yourself — You are worth your time, effort, and money. Don't let guilt enter into your head and tell yourself that you have better things to do or that you shouldn't spend the money on yourself. Guilt is one of the biggest energy suckers.

Support Your Emotions and Spritually

Now that you know how to balance your chakras, your energy will fluctuate less; you will no longer be at the mercy of having extreme peaks and valleys of emotions. You will feel peaceful for extended periods. Your feelings will no longer overwhelm you. You will be connected to your soul and in touch with your feelings. You will have more smiles than frowns.

Mantras are small phrases to remind you of who you are and why you are here. They are encouraging and motivating words. Mantras are easy to develop. Once you have written your mantra, say it often. Mantras do not have to be long or complicated. Just a few words will do. If you need help coming up with a mantra, the method I use is to take what is bothering me and use the opposite words for positive outcomes. Example, "I am in a bad mood." Instead, I say "I am coming out of a bad mood."

My Personal Mantra

**I am blessed with family, friends, and clients.
I am supported and loved.
I am powerful.
I have known gifts, and there are gifts that
I have not tapped into yet.
I do my best every day to serve those
who seek my services with honesty and integrity.**

Be Aware and Conscious of Your Energy

Protect your aura so that your chakras will not wobble with inconsistent energy flow. Negativity, like a disease that can run rampant if not monitored. If you feel like you are picking up someone's negative energy, protect yourself by activating an invisible protective bubble to shield your body before negativity eats away at your aura and attacks your chakras.

Acknowledge and high-five yourself every step of your journey. Stop competing with yourself. Stop thinking you don't have enough. Stop thinking hat you are not enough. Have a positive attitude and radiate it from a place of love. Please do not look for self-validation from others; you will only be disappointed. Even when you "do" receive external validation, this kind of energy is not sustainable. You are the only one that can determine your worth and what is best for you.

When Your Energy is Strong

You are more powerful than you believe! Do you feel overall stronger, lighter and healthier? Can you feel your inner strength radiating from your soul? Have you noticed that you want to try new things and go to new places? The emotions that have held you back were your fears and limited beliefs; now is the time to spread your wings and try new things.

STOP putting limitations on your life!

Which dialogue runs through your head? Have you begun to be aware of the useless thoughts that run through your mind and the destructive conversations that you have with yourself? These thoughts only get in the way of your progress and don't serve your higher purpose.

Challenges - As your chakras become balanced, you will find inner peace and stability. At the same time, you will begin to attract new opportunities and new people into your life. Meeting challenges are ways of telling you that your energy field is expanding and is ready for more invigorating experiences--like taking that job promotion or looking for a new job, moving to a place where you don't know anyone, or going back to school.

Yes, you will be nervous and anxious about the changes, but you need new experiences to grow and expand your chakras while preparing you for significant growth to fulfill your life purpose.

Always trust your inner instinct. It never steers you wrong unless you let doubt and fear WIN!

Instead of seeking validation elsewhere, listen and honor yourself.

This is POWER!

You are your own best friend!

What If I Can't Maintain What I Achieved?

As I said earlier, there is no wrong way of doing this work. We feel like there should be guidelines, but there aren't any. Growth comes from trusting how you feel and not be afraid to take the next step. Freedom like this will scare many people who want to know how they should feel, what to do, or what to expect.

What if you have the freedom to explore whatever you want? Without judgment, guidelines or limitations? Will it feel like free falling? Yes, it will feel daunting for a while until you learn how to land on your feet by trusting and having faith. As you master each lesson of your journey, the universe continues to give you new lessons to prepare you for your next stage of your spiritual evolution. Personal growth can only take place after you leave your comfort zone.

On your journey, there will be days when you are distracted and want to take a less stressful route. Too many people give up on their journey when they realize how hard transformation is. Why is transformation so hard? We RESIST change. Change is frightening! Suffering is comforting because we know it so well. We live in pain because we are taught that suffering is acceptable and to receive our rewards we must work hard to obtain them. Just imagine if we never change or challenged, where would we be? Probably living in a world without progress and in still in the Dark Ages.

The universe is on your side and wants to help you build your energetic muscles so that you can have what you want out of life and to maintain what you have achieved.

Yes, it takes a lot of courage and perseverance to travel this road.

Only you can choose which life is better for you!

Give yourself grace. Grace is accepting your situation for what it is. You can change direction on your path at any time. Whichever one you choose, don't judge yourself harshly and don't be afraid to make mistakes. Be the navigator of your life.

Will doubts set in? Of course they will. You are heading into unexplored territory. These feelings are real especially if you are the first in your family to break a generational pattern and do something differently. Don't let your doubts and other people's misgivings win and prevent you from continuing on your journey. I believe there is nothing worse than to be at the end of your life asking yourself, "What if I could have? or Why didn't I?"

Pick yourself up and start again, even if you have done it many times already (thank goodness for do-overs.) Your spirit will never stop calling you to step up. You can put your calling on hold, or postpone it, dim it, or decide to ***let it burn bright and loud***. You are the only one who can control your flame.

Protect Your Precious Energy Resources

This is my list of how I protect my energy resources. Please add yours to the list.

Protection Bubble — Envision putting yourself in a protective bubble upon awakening. This bubble will protect your aura and keep it close to your body for protection.

- Honor yourself in everything you do.
- Made a mistake? Acknowledge it and move on.
- Be aware of your negative thoughts so they do not overtake you.
- Keep yourself healthy. Eliminate destructive habits.
- Decide whom you want to spend your time with. Avoid gossiping, venting, and complaining.

- Don't sabotage yourself by allowing yourself to fail. Make a plan and stick to it.
- Check in with yourself and clear any negative energy.
- Minimize negativity contact.
- Don't consciously give away your power, and don't let anyone take it!

All About You Homework

What do you like about yourself?

_____

_____

_____

How do you honor yourself?

_____

_____

_____

How do you reward yourself?

_____

_____

_____

What are your favorite activities?

_____

_____

_____

Who do you love sharing life with?

_____

_____

_____

What is about yourself that you are the most proud of?

_____

_____

_____

Honoring You Meditation

This meditation honors who you are. You are the most incredible person in your life. I celebrate you. I celebrate me. I am thankful you have allowed me to accompany you on your journey and thank you for accompanying me on mine. This meditation is to feel your powers without adjusting energy levels. Honor yourself by accepting and acknowledging who you are. Just the way you are. Beautiful and empowerful!

Honoring you!

Preparation for this meditation is the same as the grounding and cleansing meditation at the beginning of this lesson.

Listen to the meditation here: http://bit.ly/2B0Ok8f

Password: Dream

Take three cleansing breaths from your diaphragm.

First or Root Chakra

Place a hand on each hip. Take a breath through your nose and exhale from your mouth. As you exhale, push the air out and drive the energy down to your hands. Relax. Feel the front of the first chakra and then the back of the chakra. Be aware of the energy. Make no adjustment. You are already powerful. Sit quietly and just feel.

Take three cleansing breaths.

Second or Emotion Chakra

Bring your hands up and place them on your second chakra, underneath your belly button. Take a breath and exhale until you feel the breath touching your hands. Take note of the energy from the front of your body then to the back. Feel how powerful and balanced this energy is, and how good you feel to be in your body.

Take three cleansing breaths.

Third or Self-Esteem Chakra

Bring your hands up and place them on your third chakra, underneath your rib cage. Take a breath in, and then drive air out through your mouth and feel it on your hands. Feel your self-esteem, your power chakra, starting in the front of your body, and then in the back. Note how this energy feels.

Everything feels good and safe in your world. You have control of your situations. Feel your power without seeking outside advice. Did you feel the shift?

Take three cleansing breaths.

Fourth or Heart Chakra

Bring your hands up and place them on your heart chakra. Take a breath in, and then exhale through your mouth until you feel the exhaled air touching your hands. Find your heartbeat. Note the vibration and the gentle beating of your heart. Can you feel the love you have for yourself? Doesn't it feel lovely? Can you feel the love you have for others too? Just feel your heart from the front of the body and then the back of the chakra. Does it feel balance to you?

Fifth or Throat Chakra

Envision bringing your hands up and placing them on your throat chakra while your hands rest in your lap. Take a breath in, and then exhale from your mouth until you feel your breath touching your hands. Feel how powerful your throat is. Feel from the front of your chakra, and then the back of the neck. It is time to let go of the pain. Let go of the painful emotion. Let go of the insecurities, because you're already so incredibly powerful. Let those words out.

Take three cleansing breaths.

Sixth or Third Eye Chakra

 Envision placing your hands on your third eye, between the eyebrows, while your hands rest in your lap. Take a breath in, and out. Feel that energy circulating from the front of the third eye chakra then to the back. Your third eye is your knowing eye, the eye behind your physical eyes that is insightful, that wants to guide you. Don't be afraid to take its advice. It wants to be your friend and help you on this journey. Shake off whatever you think you don't deserve. Instead, focus on what you have achieved and still desired.

Take three cleansing breaths.

Seventh or Crown Chakra

 If you can, place both hands on your crown chakra. If not, place them in your lap while envisioning your hands on your crown. Breathe in, and exhale from the mouth; repeat two more times. If you desire, you can circulate the energy in your crown chakra by slowly moving one hand in a circular motion above your head until you can feel the energy is moving. On the next breath, exhale and imagine your breath going from your crown down to your first chakra.

Sit quietly for a few minutes until you feel settled.

Take three cleansing breaths.

When you are ready, slowly open your eyes and get a drink of water. How do you feel? Do you feel your chakras moving at a comfortable pace?

Verygood!

Thankyou for being you!

Congratulations for Taking a Courageous Step to Make a Positive Life Change!

I want to thank you for reading *Know Your Chakras- Introduction to Energy Medicine.* I know you have learned many methods to eliminate blockages from your life. Now you can correct energy imbalances, and to remove deficiencies to attract good health, love, and positive experiences. It took tremendous amount of courage, commitment, and time to do the practices in this book to make significant life changes.

Everyone is capable of doing this work, and no one is exempt from this work. You, too, can find happiness and peace! Life can be lackluster when living with stress and the same routines! I think healthy stress is good and can be a catalyst for growth. Stress can be a powerful motivational tool when the discomforts in your life have long outlived their usefulness.

Now that you have finished the book, the real work begins. *You have just learned the skills of an energy apprentice.* You must practice these skills daily until you can master your energy with ease. This practice takes years of discipline and mindfulness. When I started my journey in 2004, I was so unaware of my being that I was continuously getting sick. I now know that these sicknesses were due to energy depletion and the absorption of psyche debris from my work environment and extended family.

Today, I am in a good place where I rarely get sick. If I do, I know how to locate, address deficient energies, and correct them immediately. As I progress on my journey, I have found peace and can live in a state of joy and peace 95% of the time. When I started my journey, I had no idea how to be consistently upbeat; stress was overwhelming me, and my ability to manage stress was non-existent.

I was dissatisfied with everything, even though I had every life's comfort I still felt empty and unhappy. Through this incredible work, I now have a range of emotions, instead of dwelling on two primary emotions, anger and emptiness. I am happy and feel good about myself, and I am helping others to learn how to heal their physical and emotional conditions while connecting with their souls. For years my happiness was depended on other people's approval, or I bought stuff that I don't need. Or I busy my life with hobbies so that I didn't have to check in with myself. Now my happiness radiates from within me instead of from external stuff.

This is what I call **FREEDOM**. I am no longer chained to what people think of me. You, too, can have the same freedom!

I commend you, and I applaud you.

You did a super job!

Need Support?

How can I support you after the book?

Schedule an in-person, Skype, or phone session – I offer many types of services, including hands-on healing, remote healing, and spiritual coaching. For more details on what I offer, please visit my website http://healingplacemedfield.com.

Participate in the Healing Place's webinars – Join me for my webinars on various energy subjects. I also take suggestions for future topics. To learn more, please watch for details on HealingPlaceEnergySchool.com and subscribe to my newsletter.

Join a class - In addition to this book, you may take the accompanying online class *Chakras 101: Know Your Energy.* This is a nine-part class series that will come to your computer over a five week period. Many of the important points in this book are discussed, along with the homework assignments in detail, and I will guide you through the healing meditations.

I am in the process of developing more online classes for Healing Place Energy School ! Join me in the coming years for:

- Holistic Digestive Health
- Keep Your Energy Healthy
- Keep Your Energy Powerful and Flowing
- Self-care Reflexology classes, and a lot more.

For more information about classes, visit
www.HealingPlaceEnergySchool.com

Guest Speaking or Motivational Speaking Opportunities – If you would like for me to speak at your next conference, please contact me at
support@HealingPlaceEnergySchool.com

Stay connected! Keep up to date with my latest news, tips and offerings by:

- Subscribing to my newsletter at www.HealingPlaceEnergySchool.com.
- My newsletters contain helpful health tips, healthy recipes, new products, services, and classes.

Follow me on

- Facebook - Facebook.com/HealingPlaceEnergySchool
- Twitter - Twitter.com/healingplacemed
- Instagram (Instagram.com/HealingPlaceEnergySchool)
- Healing Place's YouTube.com/reflexologyhealing - We have more than 200 self-help, inspirational, and meditation videos and new videos are added.

Contact me!

Email me at support@HealingPlaceEnergySchool.com

Pick up the phone and call 508-359-6463 US

Credits

Artwork by Kelly Brown - See Kelly's incredible art work on her Facebook wall (facebook.com/KStarSpangled)

Her email address is k.starspangled.illustrations@gmail.com

Editors:

Amanda Lohnes of the Healing Place LLC

Wiley McCarthy wileymcc@comcast.net, LinkedIn

Layout:

Connie Dunn, Publish with Connie http://publishwithconnie.com (publishwithconnie@gmail.com) 508-446-1711

About the Healing Place Energy School LLC

The Healing Place Energy School LLC established in 2017 by Certified Energy Medicine practitioner, Certified Reflexologist, Usui Reiki Master/Teacher Helen Chin Lui. As much as Helen enjoys working with clients, people have asked her to share her knowledge on a global platform. By establishing an online, Healing Place Energy School LLC, she shares her knowledge with anyone that has a desire to be proactive with their health care. Helen develops self-healing classes that are easy to understand and can be implemented anywhere and with the powers of your healing hands.

About the Healing Place LLC

The Healing Place LLC offers healing services to all ages who are seriously committed to breaking their cycles and patterns of pain and negativity associated with chronic digestive problems, chronic pain, and aid in natural hormonal balancing. We are pleased and honored to help thousands of clients to feel better since 2006.

We offer:

- In-person healing, Reflexology, Reiki, and Energy Medicine or Chakra Balancing.
- Skype healing and coaching sessions
- Remote healing
- Wellness and Spiritual coaching
- Self-healing classes in Reiki, Reflexology, and Energy Medicine, either in-person or online

See www.HealingPlaceMedfield.com for more details on our services.

Helen working in collaboration with
book manager Connie Dunn

Tito, Milo, and Kirby

About Helen

Helen is a Certified Reflexologist, Certified Energy Medicine Practitioner, Certified Usui Master Reiki Practitioner/Teacher with 20 years of cumulative knowledge of alternative healing methods. She is dedicated to helping her clients find long-term relief from their chronic digestive problems, chronic pain, and hormonal issues. When Helen isn't helping clients directly, she is researching and writing to expand her knowledge, so that she can educate her clients and readers about how to improve their health.

In addition to working at her office, Helen teaches self-healing classes in-person and online and attends conferences as a health motivational speaker. If you would like Helen to teach Introduction to Energy Medicine or a Hand Reflexology class at your organization or workplace, or if you would like her to speak at your next conference, please contact her at support@HealingPlaceEnergySchool.com

Helen has authored a children's book *Through My Mommy's Bellybutton*. You can find this book on Amazon.com

Healing Place Energy School LLC
and
Healing Place LLC
50 North Street
Medfield, MA 02052 US

508-359-6463
Support@HealingPlaceEnergySchool.com
HealingPlaceEnergySchool.com
HealingPlaceMedfield.com

Testimonials

Helen Chin Lui has written a thoughtful introduction to the study of how our chakras affect our physical, emotional, and spiritual health. Her guided meditations and written assignments provide valuable tools for those seeking to support their health through non-traditional medical practices. By sharing not only her own stories, but also those of reflexology clients, she demonstrates the power of her healing techniques. A very good way to start your journey to a better YOU! - Wiley, Wellesley, MA

What a great class! I learned so much about chakras and auras. I had heard of those terms but didn't know what they meant until this course. I look forward to reviewing the material over again. Once Chakra 201 comes out I'll be all in again. Helen's voice is such a soothing balm to a stressful world. Thank you Helen! I highly recommend this class. It will improve your quality of life. Many blessings to all. - Lina Mateus

Chakra 101- "Know Your Energy" was very informative and well presented by Helen Chin Lui. She explains all the seven chakras and has charts that coincide. She brings you to a calm and quiet place before the meditations, which are a perfect way to end each session. I would recommend this course to further extend your knowledge on Chakras and how they relate to energy in the body. - Kristen K.

Made in the USA
Columbia, SC
03 September 2018